The Constitution
of the Republic of Kosovo:
Europe's Newest Nation

English Edition

Prepared and Introduced by
Yusuf Hashani

CS Publishing, 2018

Contents

Map: Kosovo and the Region

Introduction

The Constitution of Kosovo (or Kosova), refers to the supreme law (article 16) of the Republic of Kosovo. Article four of the constitution establishes the rules and separate powers of the three branches of the government.

Only two months after the independence of Kosovo itself, the constitution was signed on the 7th of April, 2008, at the national library in Prishtina. The constitution was ratified on 9th of April and came to effect on the 15th of June, 2008.[1]

This English edition of the document, with an Introduction, Map, and Transliteration Chart will give the reader a general overview of the laws and the governing body of this new country in the heart of Europe aspiring to soon join the EU.

---

[1] For more on the history of Kosovo, see *Kosovo: What Everyone Needs to Know* by Tim Judah, and *Kosovo: A Short History* by Noel Malcolm.

Common Political Acronyms in Kosovo

AAK	Aleanca për Ardhmërinë e Kosovës (Alliance for the Future of Kosovo)
ADK	Alternativa Demokrative e Kosovës (Democratic Alternative of Kosovo)
AFK	Alliance for the Future of Kosovo
AKM	Agjencia Kosovare e Mirëbesimit (Kosovo Trust Agency)
AKR	Aleanca Kosova e Re (Alliance for a New Kosovo)
AKSH	Armata Kombëtare Shqiptare (Albanian National Army)
ASHAK	Akademia e Shkencave dhe e Arteve e Kosovës (Academy of Sciences and Arts of Kosovo)
ATP	Autonomous Trade Preference
BK	Balli Kombëtar (National Front)
BSDAK	Bošnjacka Stranka Demokratske Akcije Kosovo (Bosnian Democratic Action Party of Kosovo)
BSPK	Bashkimi i Sindikatave të Pavarura të Kosovës (Independent Trade Union Confederation of Kosovo)
CBK	Central Bank of Kosovo
CEFTA	Central European Free Trade Agreement
DLK	Democratic League of Kosovo
EU	European Union
EULEX	European Union Rule of Law Mission in Kosovo
EUMIK	European Union Mission in Kosovo
EUSR	European Union Special Representative
FRY	Federal Republic of Yugoslavia
FSK	Forca e Sigurisë së Kosovës (Kosovo Security Force)
IRDK	Iniciativa e Re Demokratike e Kosovës (New Initiative for a Democratic Kosovo)
KAN	Kosovo Action Network
KDOM	Kosovo Diplomatic Observer Mission

KDTP	Kosovo Demokratik Türk Partisi (Turkish Democratic Party of Kosovo)
KLA	Kosovo Liberation Army
KJC	Kosovo Judicial Council
KMLDNJ	Këshilli për Mbrojtjen e të Drejtave dhe të Lirive të Njeriut (Council for the Defense of Human Rights and Freedoms)
KP	Kosovo Police
KTA	Kosovo Trust Agency
LBD	Lëvizja e Bashkuar Demokratike (United Democratic Movement)
LDK	Lidhja Demokratike e Kosovës (Democratic League of Kosovo)
LPK	Lëvizja Popullore e Kosovës (Kosovo People's Movement)
NATO	North Atlantic Treaty Organization
OSCE	Organization for Security and Cooperation in Europe
PAK	Privatisation Agency of Kosovo
PBD	Partia e Bashkimit Demokratik (Democratic Union
PD	Partia e Drejtësisë (Justice Party)
PDK	Partia Demokratike e Kosovës (Democratic Party of
PGJK	Partia e të Gjelbërve të Kosovës (Green Party of Kosovo)
PLK	Partia Liberale e Kosovës (Liberal Party of Kosovo)
UÇK	Ushtria Çlirimtare e Kosovës (Kosovo Liberation Army)
UN	United Nations
UNESCO	United Nations Educational, Scientific and Cultural
UNHCR	United Nations High Commissioner for Refugees
UNMIK	United Nations Interim Admin. in Kosovo

The Albanian Alphabet & Transliteration Chart

Letters		Read as	Pronounce	Albanian Examples	English equivalent
A	a	a	a	af<u>ë</u>r	f<u>a</u>r
B	b	bë	b	buk<u>ë</u>	<u>b</u>at
C	c	c<u>ë</u>	ts	ceremoni	i<u>ts</u>y
Ç	ç	<u>ç</u>ë	tʃ	<u>ç</u>el<u>ë</u>s	<u>ch</u>at
D	d	d<u>ë</u>	d	das<u>ë</u>m	<u>d</u>oor
Dh	dh	dh<u>ë</u>	ð	dhelp<u>ë</u>r	<u>th</u>ere
E	e	e	e	em<u>ë</u>r	<u>e</u>nter
Ë	ë	<u>ë</u>	ə	<u>ë</u>mb<u>ë</u>l	<u>a</u>round
F	f	f<u>ë</u>	f	flet<u>ë</u>	<u>f</u>ly
G	g	g<u>ë</u>	g	gur<u>ë</u>	<u>g</u>um
Gj	gj	gj<u>ë</u>	ɟ	gjeneral	<u>j</u>oin
H	h	h<u>ë</u>	h	hap	<u>h</u>at
I	i	i	i	ilaç	s<u>ea</u>
J	j	j<u>ë</u>	j	jav<u>ë</u>	<u>y</u>awn
K	k	k<u>ë</u>	k	k<u>ë</u>mish<u>ë</u>	<u>k</u>ite
L	l	l<u>ë</u>	l	lop<u>ë</u>	<u>l</u>eave
Ll	ll	ll<u>ë</u>	ł or l	llamp<u>ë</u>	mi<u>ll</u>
M	m	m<u>ë</u>	m	mal	<u>m</u>an
N	n	n<u>ë</u>	n	n<u>ë</u>n<u>ë</u>	<u>n</u>o
Nj	nj	nj<u>ë</u>	ɲ	njeri	o<u>ni</u>on
O	o	o	o	or<u>ë</u>	<u>o</u>pen
P	p	p<u>ë</u>	p	parti	<u>p</u>en
Q	q	q<u>ë</u>	q	<u>q</u>um<u>ë</u>sht	ma<u>t</u>ure

R	**r**	r<u>ë</u>	ɾ	raport	<u>r</u>ed
Rr	**rr**	rr<u>ë</u>	r (rolled)	rrjesht	bo<u>rr</u>ow
S	**s**	s<u>ë</u>	s	stacion	<u>s</u>top
Sh	**sh**	sh<u>ë</u>	ʃ	shtëpi	<u>sh</u>op
T	**t**	t<u>ë</u>	t	televizion	<u>t</u>ree
Th	**th**	th<u>ë</u>	θ	thupër	<u>th</u>in
U	**u**	u	u	ur<u>ë</u>	f<u>oo</u>d
V	**v**	v<u>ë</u>	v	vez<u>ë</u>	<u>v</u>est
X	**x**	x<u>ë</u>	dz	xix<u>ë</u>	ad<u>ze</u>
Xh	**xh**	xh<u>ë</u>	dʒ	xhaxha	<u>J</u>upiter
Y	**y**	y	y	yll	n<u>ew</u>*
Z	**z**	z	z	zem<u>ë</u>r	<u>z</u>ebra
Zh	**zh**	zh<u>ë</u>	ʒ	zhurm<u>ë</u>	plea<u>s</u>ure

*No English equivalent found.

THE CONSTITUTION OF THE REPUBLIC OF KOSOVO

We, the people of Kosovo,

Determined to build a future of Kosovo as a free, democratic and peace-loving country that will be a homeland to all of its citizens;

Committed to the creation of a state of free citizens that will guarantee the rights of every citizen, civil freedoms and equality of all citizens before the law;

Committed to the state of Kosovo as a state of economic wellbeing and social prosperity;

Convinced that the state of Kosovo will contribute to the stability of the region and entire Europe by creating relations of good neighborliness and cooperation with all neighboring countries;

Convinced that the state of Kosovo will be a dignified member of the family of peace-loving states in the world;

With the intention of having the state of Kosovo fully participating in the processes of Euro-Atlantic integration;

In a solemn manner, we approve the Constitution of the Republic of Kosovo.

Chapter I Basic Provisions

Article 1   [Definition of State]

1. The Republic of Kosovo is an independent, sovereign, democratic, unique and indivisible state.

2. The Republic of Kosovo is a state of its citizens. The Republic of Kosovo exercises its authority based on the respect for human rights and freedoms of its citizens and all other individuals within its borders.

3. The Republic of Kosovo shall have no territorial claims against, and shall seek no union with, any State or part of any State.

Article 2   [Sovereignty]

1. The sovereignty of the Republic of Kosovo stems from the people, belongs to the people and is exercised in compliance with the Constitution through elected representatives, referendum and other forms in compliance with the provisions of this Constitution.

2. The sovereignty and territorial integrity of the Republic of Kosovo is intact, inalienable, indivisible and protected by all means provided in this Constitution and the law.

3. The Republic of Kosovo, in order to maintain peace and to protect national interests, may participate in systems of international security.

Article 3   [Equality Before the Law]

1. The Republic of Kosovo is a multi-ethnic society consisting of Albanian and other Communities, governed democratically with full respect for the rule of law through its legislative, executive and judicial institutions.

2. The exercise of public authority in the Republic of Kosovo shall be based upon the principles of equality of all individuals before the law and with full respect for internationally recognized fundamental human rights and freedoms, as well as protection of the rights of and participation by all Communities and their members.

Article 4   [Form of Government and Separation of Power]

1. Kosovo is a democratic Republic based on the principle of separation of powers and the checks and balances among them as provided in this Constitution.

2. The Assembly of the Republic of Kosovo exercises the legislative power.

3. The President of the Republic of Kosovo represents the unity of the people. The President of the Republic of Kosovo is the legitimate representative of the country, internally and

externally, and is the guarantor of the democratic functioning of the institutions of the Republic of Kosovo, as provided in this Constitution.

4. The Government of the Republic of Kosovo is responsible for implementation of laws and state policies and is subject to parliamentarian control.

5. The judicial power is unique and independent and is exercised by courts.

6. The Constitutional Court is an independent organ in protecting the constitutionality and is the final interpreter of the Constitution.

7. The Republic of Kosovo has institutions for the protection of the constitutional order and territorial integrity, public order and safety, which operate under the constitutional authority of the democratic institutions of the Republic of Kosovo.

Article 5   [Languages]

1. The official languages in the Republic of Kosovo are Albanian and Serbian.

2. Turkish, Bosnian and Roma languages have the status of official languages at the municipal level or will be in official use at all levels as provided by law.

Article 6   [Symbols]

1. The flag, the seal and the anthem are the state symbols of the Republic of Kosovo all of which reflect its multi-ethnic character.

2. The appearance, display and protection of the flag and other state symbols shall be regulated by law. The display and protection of the national symbols shall be regulated by law.

Article 7   [Values]

1. The constitutional order of the Republic of Kosovo is based on the principles of freedom, peace, democracy, equality, respect for human rights and freedoms and the rule of law, non-discrimination, the right to property, the protection of environment, social justice, pluralism, separation of state powers, and a market economy.

2. The Republic of Kosovo ensures gender equality as a fundamental value for the democratic development of the society, providing equal opportunities for both female and male participation in the political, economic, social, cultural and other areas of societal life.

Article 8   [Secular State]

The Republic of Kosovo is a secular state and is neutral in matters of religious beliefs.

Article 9   [Cultural and Religious Heritage]

The Republic of Kosovo ensures the preservation and protection of its cultural and religious heritage.

Article 10   [Economy]

A market economy with free competition is the basis of the economic order of the Republic of Kosovo.

Article 11   [Currency]

1. The Republic of Kosovo uses as legal tender one single currency.

2. The Central Banking Authority of Kosovo is independent and is called the Central Bank of the Republic of Kosovo.

Article 12   [Local Government]

1. Municipalities are the basic territorial unit of local self-governance in the Republic of Kosovo.

2. The organization and powers of units of local self-government are provided by law.

Article 13   [Capital City]

1. The capital city of the Republic of Kosovo is Pristina.

2. The status and organization of the capital city is provided by law.

Article 14   [Citizenship]

The acquisition and termination of the right of citizenship of the Republic of Kosovo are provided by law.

Article 15   [Citizens Living Abroad]

The Republic of Kosovo protects the interests of its citizens abroad as provided by law.

Article 16   [Supremacy of the Constitution]

1. The Constitution is the highest legal act of the Republic of Kosovo. Laws and other legal acts shall be in accordance with this Constitution.

2. The power to govern stems from the Constitution.

3. The Republic of Kosovo shall respect international law.

4. Every person and entity in the Republic of Kosovo is subject to the provisions of the Constitution.

Article 17   [International Agreements]

1. The Republic of Kosovo concludes international agreements and becomes a member of international organizations.

2. The Republic of Kosovo participates in international cooperation for promotion and protection of peace, security and human rights.

Article 18   [Ratification of International Agreements]

1. International agreements relating to the following subjects are ratified by two thirds (2/3) vote of all deputies of the Assembly:

    (1) territory, peace, alliances, political and military issues;

    (2) fundamental rights and freedoms;

    (3) membership of the Republic of Kosovo in international organizations;

    (4) the undertaking of financial obligations by the Republic of Kosovo;

2. International agreements other than those in paragraph 1 are ratified upon signature of the President of the Republic of Kosovo.

3. The President of the Republic of Kosovo or the Prime Minister notifies the Assembly whenever an international agreement is signed.

4. Amendment of or withdrawal from international agreements follows the same decision making process as the ratification of such international agreements.

5. The principles and procedures for ratifying and contesting international agreements are set forth by law.

Article 19   [Applicability of International Law]

1. International agreements ratified by the Republic of Kosovo become part of the internal legal system after their publication in the Official Gazette of the Republic of Kosovo. They are directly applied except for cases when they are not self-applicable and the application requires the promulgation of a law.

2. Ratified international agreements and legally binding norms of international law have superiority over the laws of the Republic of Kosovo.

Article 20   [Delegation of Sovereignty]

1. The Republic of Kosovo may on the basis of ratified international agreements delegate state powers for specific matters to international organizations.

2. If a membership agreement ratified by the Republic of Kosovo for its participation in an international organization explicitly contemplates the direct applicability of the norms of that organization, then the law ratifying the international agreement must be adopted by two thirds (2/3) vote of all deputies of the Assembly, and those norms have superiority over the laws of the Republic of Kosovo.

Chapter II Fundamental Rights and Freedoms

Article 21 [General Principles]

1. Human rights and fundamental freedoms are indivisible, inalienable and inviolable and are the basis of the legal order of the Republic of Kosovo.

2. The Republic of Kosovo protects and guarantees human rights and fundamental freedoms as provided by this Constitution.

3. Everyone must respect the human rights and fundamental freedoms of others.

4. Fundamental rights and freedoms set forth in the Constitution are also valid for legal persons to the extent applicable.

Article 22 [Direct Applicability of International Agreements and Instruments]

Human rights and fundamental freedoms guaranteed by the following international agreements and instruments are guaranteed by this Constitution, are directly applicable in the Republic of Kosovo and, in the case of conflict, have priority over provisions of laws and other acts of public institutions:

(1) Universal Declaration of Human Rights;

(2) European Convention for the Protection of Human Rights and Fundamental Freedoms and its Protocols;

(3) International Covenant on Civil and Political Rights and its Protocols;

(4) Council of Europe Framework Convention for the Protection of National Minorities;

(5) Convention on the Elimination of All Forms of Racial Discrimination;

(6) Convention on the Elimination of All Forms of Discrimination Against Women;

(7) Convention on the Rights of the Child;

(8) Convention against Torture and Other Cruel, Inhumane or Degrading Treatment or Punishment;

Article 23 [Human Dignity]

Human dignity is inviolable and is the basis of all human rights and fundamental freedoms.

Article 24 [Equality Before the Law]

1. All are equal before the law. Everyone enjoys the right to equal legal protection without discrimination.

2. No one shall be discriminated against on grounds of race, color, gender, language, religion, political or other opinion, national or social origin, relation to any community, property, economic and social condition, sexual orientation, birth, disability or other personal status.

3. Principles of equal legal protection shall not prevent the imposition of measures necessary to protect and advance the rights of individuals and groups who are in unequal positions. Such measures shall be applied only until the purposes for which they are imposed have been fulfilled.

Article 25 [Right to Life]

1. Every individual enjoys the right to life.

2. Capital punishment is forbidden.

Article 26 [Right to Personal Integrity]

Every person enjoys the right to have his/her physical and psychological integrity respected, which includes:

(1) the right to make decisions in relation to reproduction in accordance with the rules and procedures set forth by law;

(2) the right to have control over her/his body in accordance with law;

(3) the right not to undergo medical treatment against his/her will as provided by law;

(4) the right not to participate in medical or scientific experiments without her/his prior consent.

Article 27 [Prohibition of Torture, Cruel, Inhuman or Degrading Treatment]

No one shall be subject to torture, cruel, inhuman or degrading treatment or punishment.

Article 28 [Prohibition of Slavery and Forced Labor]

1. No one shall be held in slavery or servitude.

2. No one shall be required to perform forced labor. Labor or services provided by law by persons convicted by a final court decision while serving their sentence or during a State

of Emergency declared in compliance with the rules set forth in this Constitution shall not be considered as forced labor.

3. Trafficking in persons is forbidden.

Article 29 [Right to Liberty and Security]

1. Everyone is guaranteed the right to liberty and security. No one shall be deprived of liberty except in the cases foreseen by law and after a decision of a competent court as follows:

    (1) pursuant to a sentence of imprisonment for committing a criminal act;

    (2) for reasonable suspicion of having committed a criminal act, only when deprivation of liberty is reasonably considered necessary to prevent commission of another criminal act, and only for a limited time before trial as provided by law;

    (3) for the purpose of educational supervision of a minor or for the purpose of bringing the minor before a competent institution in accordance with a lawful order;

    (4) for the purpose of medical supervision of a person who because of disease represents a danger to society;

    (5) for illegal entry into the Republic of Kosovo or pursuant to a lawful order of expulsion or extradition.

2. Everyone who is deprived of liberty shall be promptly informed, in a language he/she understands, of the reasons of deprivation. The written notice on the reasons of deprivation shall be provided as soon as possible. Everyone who is deprived of liberty without a court order shall be brought within forty-eight (48) hours before a judge who decides on her/his detention or release not later than forty-eight (48) hours from the moment the detained person is brought before the court. Everyone who is arrested shall be entitled to trial within a reasonable time and to release pending trial, unless the judge concludes that the person is a danger to the community or presents a substantial risk of fleeing before trial.

3. Everyone who is deprived of liberty shall be promptly informed of his/her right not to make any statements, right to defense counsel of her/his choosing, and the right to promptly communicate with a person of his/her choosing.

4. Everyone who is deprived of liberty by arrest or detention enjoys the right to use legal remedies to challenge the lawfulness of the arrest or detention. The case shall be speedily decided by a court and release shall be ordered if the arrest or detention is determined to be unlawful.

5. Everyone who has been detained or arrested in contradiction with the provisions of this article has a right to compensation in a manner provided by law.

6. An individual who is sentenced has the right to challenge the conditions of detention in a manner provided by law.

Article 30 [Rights of the Accused]

Everyone charged with a criminal offense shall enjoy the following minimum rights:

(1) to be promptly informed, in a language that she/he understands, of the nature and cause of the accusation against him/her;

(2) to be promptly informed of her/his rights according to law;

(3) to have adequate time, facilities and remedies for the preparation of his/her defense;

(4) to have free assistance of an interpreter if she/he cannot understand or speak the language used in court;

(5) to have assistance of legal counsel of his/her choosing, to freely communicate with counsel and if she/he does not have sufficient means, to be provided free counsel;

(6) to not be forced to testify against oneself or admit one's guilt.

Article 31 [Right to Fair and Impartial Trial]

1. Everyone shall be guaranteed equal protection of rights in the proceedings before courts, other state authorities and holders of public powers.

2. Everyone is entitled to a fair and impartial public hearing as to the determination of one's rights and obligations or as to any criminal charges within a reasonable time by an independent and impartial tribunal established by law.

3. Trials shall be open to the public except in limited circumstances in which the court determines that in the interest of justice the public or the media should be excluded because their presence would endanger public order, national security, the interests of minors or the privacy of parties in the process in accordance with law.

4. Everyone charged with a criminal offense has the right to examine witnesses and to obtain the obligatory attendance of witnesses, experts and other persons who may clarify the evidence.

5. Everyone charged with a criminal offense is presumed innocent until proven guilty according to law.

6. Free legal assistance shall be provided to those without sufficient financial means if such assistance is necessary to ensure effective access to justice.

7. Judicial proceedings involving minors shall be regulated by law respecting special rules and procedures for juveniles.

Article 32 [Right to Legal Remedies]

Every person has the right to pursue legal remedies against judicial and administrative decisions which infringe on his/her rights or interests, in the manner provided by law.

Article 33 [The Principle of Legality and Proportionality in Criminal Cases]

1. No one shall be charged or punished for any act which did not constitute a penal offense under law at the time it was committed, except acts that at the time they were committed constituted genocide, war crimes or crimes against humanity according to international law.

2. No punishment for a criminal act shall exceed the penalty provided by law at the time the criminal act was committed.

3. The degree of punishment cannot be disproportional to the criminal offense.

4. Punishments shall be administered in accordance with the law in force at the time a criminal act was committed, unless the penalties in a subsequent applicable law are more favorable to the perpetrator.

Article 34 [Right not to be Tried Twice for the Same Criminal Act]

No one shall be tried more than once for the same criminal act.

Article 35 [Freedom of Movement]

1. Citizens of the Republic of Kosovo and foreigners who are legal residents of Kosovo have the right to move freely throughout the Republic of Kosovo and choose their location of residence.

2. Each person has the right to leave the country. Limitations on this right may be regulated by law if they are necessary for legal proceedings, enforcement of a court decision or the performance of a national defense obligation.

3. Citizens of the Republic of Kosovo shall not be deprived the right of entry into Kosovo.

4. Citizens of the Republic of Kosovo shall not be extradited from Kosovo against their will except for cases when otherwise required by international law and agreements.

5. The right of foreigners to enter the Republic of Kosovo and reside in the country shall be defined by law.

Article 36 [Right to Privacy]

1. Everyone enjoys the right to have her/his private and family life respected, the inviolability of residence, and the confidentiality of correspondence, telecommunication and other communication.

2. Searches of any private dwelling or establishment that are deemed necessary for the investigation of a crime may be conducted only to the extent necessary and only after approval by a court after a showing of the reasons why such a search is necessary. Derogation from this rule is permitted if it is necessary for a lawful arrest, to collect evidence which might be in danger of loss or to avoid direct and serious risk to humans and property as defined by law. A court must retroactively approve such actions.

3. Secrecy of correspondence, telephony and other communication is an inviolable right. This right may only be limited temporarily by court decision if it is necessary for criminal proceedings or defense of the country as defined by law.

4. Every person enjoys the right of protection of personal data. Collection, preservation, access, correction and use of personal data are regulated by law.

Article 37   [Right to Marriage and Family]

1. Based on free will, everyone enjoys the right to marry and the right to have a family as provided by law.

2. Marriage and divorce are regulated by law and are based on the equality of spouses.

3. Family enjoys special protection by the state in a manner provided by law.

Article 38   [Freedom of Belief, Conscience and Religion]

1. Freedom of belief, conscience and religion is guaranteed.

2. Freedom of belief, conscience and religion includes the right to accept and manifest religion, the right to express personal beliefs and the right to accept or refuse membership in a religious community or group.

3. No one shall be required to practice or be prevented from practicing religion nor shall anyone be required to make his/her opinions and beliefs public.

4. Freedom of manifesting religion, beliefs and conscience may be limited by law if it is necessary to protect public safety and order or the health or rights of other persons.

Article 39   [Religious Denominations]

1. The Republic of Kosovo ensures and protects religious autonomy and religious monuments within its territory.

2. Religious denominations are free to independently regulate their internal organization, religious activities and religious ceremonies.

3. Religious denominations have the right to establish religious schools and charity institutions in accordance with this Constitution and the law.

Article 40 [Freedom of Expression]

1. Freedom of expression is guaranteed. Freedom of expression includes the right to express oneself, to disseminate and receive information, opinions and other messages without impediment.

2. The freedom of expression can be limited by law in cases when it is necessary to prevent encouragement or provocation of violence and hostility on grounds of race, nationality, ethnicity or religion.

Article 41 [Right of Access to Public Documents]

1. Every person enjoys the right of access to public documents.

2. Documents of public institutions and organs of state authorities are public, except for information that is limited by law due to privacy, business trade secrets or security classification.

Article 42 [Freedom of Media]

1. Freedom and pluralism of media is guaranteed.

2. Censorship is forbidden. No one shall prevent the dissemination of information or ideas through media, except if it is necessary to prevent encouragement or provocation of violence and hostility on grounds of race, nationality, ethnicity or religion.

3. Everyone has the right to correct untrue, incomplete and inaccurate published information, if it violates her/his rights and interests in accordance with the law.

Article 43 [Freedom of Gathering]

Freedom of peaceful gathering is guaranteed. Every person has the right to organize gatherings, protests and demonstrations and the right to participate in them. These rights may be limited by law, if it is necessary to safeguard public order, public health, national security or the protection of the rights of others.

Article 44 [Freedom of Association]

1. The freedom of association is guaranteed. The freedom of association includes the right of everyone to establish an organization without obtaining any permission, to be or not to be a member of any organization and to participate in the activities of an organization.

2. The freedom to establish trade unions and to organize with the intent to protect interests is guaranteed. This right may be limited by law for specific categories of employees.

3. Organizations or activities that infringe on the constitutional order, violate human rights and freedoms or encourage racial, national, ethnic or religious hatred may be prohibited by a decision of a competent court.

Article 45 [Freedom of Election and Participation]

1. Every citizen of the Republic of Kosovo who has reached the age of eighteen, even if on the day of elections, has the right to elect and be elected, unless this right is limited by a court decision.

2. The vote is personal, equal, free and secret.

3. State institutions support the possibility of every person to participate in public activities and everyone's right to democratically influence decisions of public bodies.

Article 46 [Protection of Property]

1. The right to own property is guaranteed.

2. Use of property is regulated by law in accordance with the public interest.

3. No one shall be arbitrarily deprived of property. The Republic of Kosovo or a public authority of the Republic of Kosovo may expropriate property if such expropriation is authorized by law, is necessary or appropriate to the achievement of a public purpose or the promotion of the public interest, and is followed by the provision of immediate and adequate compensation to the person or persons whose property has been expropriated.

4. Disputes arising from an act of the Republic of Kosovo or a public authority of the Republic of Kosovo that is alleged to constitute an expropriation shall be settled by a competent court.

5. Intellectual property is protected by law.

Article 47 [Right to Education]

1. Every person enjoys the right to free basic education. Mandatory education is regulated by law and funded by public funds.

2. Public institutions shall ensure equal opportunities to education for everyone in accordance with their specific abilities and needs.

Article 48 [Freedom of Art and Science]

1. The freedom of artistic and scientific creativity is guaranteed.

2. Academic freedom is guaranteed.

Article 49 [Right to Work and Exercise Profession]

1. The right to work is guaranteed.

2. Every person is free to choose his/her profession and occupation.

Article 50 [Rights of Children]

1. Children enjoy the right to protection and care necessary for their wellbeing.

2. Children born out of wedlock have equal rights to those born in marriage.

3. Every child enjoys the right to be protected from violence, maltreatment and exploitation.

4. All actions undertaken by public or private authorities concerning children shall be in the best interest of the children.

5. Every child enjoys the right to regular personal relations and direct contact with parents, unless a competent institution determines that this is in contradiction with the best interest of the child.

Article 51 [Health and Social Protection]

1. Healthcare and social insurance are regulated by law.

2. Basic social insurance related to unemployment, disease, disability and old age shall be regulated by law.

Article 52 [Responsibility for the Environment]

1. Nature and biodiversity, environment and national inheritance are everyone's responsibility.

2. Everyone should be provided an opportunity to be heard by public institutions and have their opinions considered on issues that impact the environment in which they live.

3. The impact on the environment shall be considered by public institutions in their decision making processes.

Article 53 [Interpretation of Human Rights Provisions]

Human rights and fundamental freedoms guaranteed by this Constitution shall be interpreted consistent with the court decisions of the European Court of Human Rights.

Article 54 [Judicial Protection of Rights]

Everyone enjoys the right of judicial protection if any right guaranteed by this Constitution or by law has been violated or denied and has the right to an effective legal remedy if found that such right has been violated.

Article 55 [Limitations on Fundamental Rights and Freedoms]

1. Fundamental rights and freedoms guaranteed by this Constitution may only be limited by law.

2. Fundamental rights and freedoms guaranteed by this Constitution may be limited to the extent necessary for the fulfillment of the purpose of the limitation in an open and democratic society.

3. Fundamental rights and freedoms guaranteed by this Constitution may not be limited for purposes other than those for which they were provided.

4. In cases of limitations of human rights or the interpretation of those limitations; all public authorities, and in particular courts, shall pay special attention to the essence of the right limited, the importance of the purpose of the limitation, the nature and extent of the limitation, the relation between the limitation and the purpose to be achieved and the review of the possibility of achieving the purpose with a lesser limitation.

5. The limitation of fundamental rights and freedoms guaranteed by this Constitution shall in no way deny the essence of the guaranteed right.

Article 56 [Fundamental Rights and Freedoms During a State of Emergency]

1. Derogation of the fundamental rights and freedoms protected by this Constitution may only occur following the declaration of a State of Emergency as provided by this Constitution and only to the extent necessary under the relevant circumstances.

2. Derogation of the fundamental rights and freedoms guaranteed by Articles 23, 24, 25, 27, 28, 29, 31, 33, 34, 37 and 38 of this Constitution shall not be permitted under any circumstances.

Chapter III   Rights of Communities and Their Members

Article 57   [General Principles]

1. Inhabitants belonging to the same national or ethnic, linguistic, or religious group traditionally present on the territory of the Republic of Kosovo (Communities) shall have specific rights as set forth in this Constitution in addition to the human rights and fundamental freedoms provided in chapter II of this Constitution.

2. Every member of a community shall have the right to freely choose to be treated or not to be treated as such and no discrimination shall result from this choice or from the exercise of the rights that are connected to that choice.

3. Members of Communities shall have the right to freely express, foster and develop their identity and community attributes.

4. The exercise of these rights shall carry with it duties and responsibilities to act in accordance with the law of the Republic of Kosovo and shall not violate the rights of others.

Article 58   [Responsibilities of the State]

1. The Republic of Kosovo ensures appropriate conditions enabling communities, and their members to preserve, protect and develop their identities. The Government shall particularly support cultural initiatives from communities and their members, including through financial assistance.

2. The Republic of Kosovo shall promote a spirit of tolerance, dialogue and support reconciliation among communities and respect the standards set forth in the Council of Europe Framework Convention for the Protection of National Minorities and the European Charter for Regional or Minority Languages.

3. The Republic of Kosovo shall take all necessary measures to protect persons who may be subject to threats or acts of discrimination, hostility or violence as a result of their national, ethnic, cultural, linguistic or religious identity.

4. The Republic of Kosovo shall adopt adequate measures as may be necessary to promote, in all areas of economic, social, political and cultural life, full and effective equality among members of communities. Such measures shall not be considered to be an act of discrimination.

5. The Republic of Kosovo shall promote the preservation of the cultural and religious heritage of all communities as an integral part of the heritage of Kosovo. The Republic of Kosovo shall have a special duty to ensure an effective protection of the entirety of sites and monuments of cultural and religious significance to the communities.

6. The Republic of Kosovo shall take effective actions against all those undermining the enjoyment of the rights of members of Communities. The Republic of Kosovo shall refrain from policies or practices aimed at assimilation of persons belonging to Communities against their will, and shall protect these persons from any action aimed at such assimilation.

7. The Republic of Kosovo ensures, on a non-discriminatory basis, that all communities and their members may exercise their rights specified in this Constitution.

Article 59 [Rights of Communities and their Members]

Members of communities shall have the right, individually or in community, to:

(1) express, maintain and develop their culture and preserve the essential elements of their identity, namely their religion, language, traditions and culture;

(2) receive public education in one of the official languages of the Republic of Kosovo of their choice at all levels;

(3) receive pre-school, primary and secondary public education, in their own language to the extent prescribed by law, with the thresholds for establishing specific classes or schools for this purpose being lower than normally stipulated for educational institutions;

(4) establish and manage their own private educational and training establishments for which public financial assistance may be granted, in accordance with the law and international standards;

(5) use their language and alphabet freely in private and in public;

(6) Use their language and alphabet in their relations with the municipal authorities or local offices of central authorities in areas where they represent a sufficient share of the population in accordance with the law. The costs incurred by the use of an interpreter or a translator shall be borne by the competent authorities;

(7) use and display community symbols, in accordance with the law and international standards;

(8) have personal names registered in their original form and in the script of their language as well as revert to original names that have been changed by force;

(9) have local names, street names and other topographical indications which reflect and are sensitive to the multi-ethnic and multi-linguistic character of the area at issue;

(10) have guaranteed access to, and special representation in, public broadcast media as well as programming in their language, in accordance with the law and international standards;

(11) to create and use their own media, including to provide information in their language through, among others, daily newspapers and wire services and the use of a reserved number of frequencies for electronic media in accordance with the law and international standards. The Republic of Kosovo shall take all measures necessary to secure an international frequency plan to allow the Kosovo Serb Community access to a licensed Kosovo-wide independent Serbian language television channel;

(12) enjoy unhindered contacts among themselves within the Republic of Kosovo and establish and maintain free and peaceful contacts with persons in any State, in particular those with whom they share an ethnic, cultural, linguistic or religious identity, or a common cultural heritage, in accordance with the law and international standards;

(13) enjoy unhindered contacts with, and participate without discrimination in the activities of local, regional and international non-governmental organizations;

(14) establish associations for culture, art, science and education as well as scholarly and other associations for the expression, fostering and development of their identity.

Article 60 [Consultative Council for Communities]

1. A Consultative Council for Communities acts under the authority of the President of the Republic of Kosovo in which all Communities shall be represented.

2. The Consultative Council for Communities shall be composed, among others, of representatives of associations of Communities.

3. The mandate of the Consultative Council for Communities shall:

(1) provide a mechanism for regular exchange between the Communities and the Government of Kosovo.

(2) afford to the Communities the opportunity to comment at an early stage on legislative or policy initiatives that may be prepared by the Government, to suggest such initiatives, and to seek to have their views incorporated in the relevant projects and programs.

(3) have any other responsibilities and functions as provided in accordance with law.

Article 61 [Representation in Public Institutions Employment]

Communities and their members shall be entitled to equitable representation in employment in public bodies and publicly owned enterprises at all levels, including in particular in the police service in areas inhabited by the respective Community, while respecting the rules concerning competence and integrity that govern public administration.

Article 62 [Representation in the Institutions of Local Government]

1. In municipalities where at least ten per cent (10%) of the residents belong to Communities not in the majority in those municipalities, a post of Vice President of the Municipal Assembly for Communities shall be reserved for a representative of these communities.

2. The position of Vice President shall be held by the non-majority candidate who received the most votes on the open list of candidates for election to the Municipal Assembly.

3. The Vice President for Communities shall promote inter-Community dialogue and serve as formal focal point for addressing non-majority Communities' concerns and interests in meetings of the Assembly and its work. The Vice President shall also be responsible for reviewing claims by Communities or their members that the acts or decisions of the Municipal Assembly violate their constitutionally guaranteed rights. The Vice President shall refer such matters to the Municipal Assembly for its reconsideration of the act or decision.

4. In the event the Municipal Assembly chooses not to reconsider its act or decision, or the Vice President deems the result, upon reconsideration, to still present a violation of a constitutionally guaranteed right, the Vice President may submit the matter directly to the Constitutional Court, which may decide whether or not to accept the matter for review.

5. In these municipalities, representation for non-majority Communities in the Republic of Kosovo in the municipal executive body is guaranteed.

Chapter IV   Assembly of the Republic of Kosovo

Article 63   [General Principles]

The Assembly is the legislative institution of the Republic of Kosovo directly elected by the people.

Article 64   [Structure of Assembly]

1. The Assembly has one hundred twenty (120) deputies elected by secret ballot on the basis of open lists. The seats in the Assembly are distributed amongst all parties, coalitions, citizens' initiatives and independent candidates in proportion to the number of valid votes received by them in the election to the Assembly.

2. In the framework of this distribution, twenty (20) of the one hundred twenty (120) seats are guaranteed for representation of communities that are not in the majority in Kosovo as follows:

   (1) Parties, coalitions, citizens' initiatives and independent candidates having declared themselves representing the Kosovo Serb Community shall have the total number of seats won through the open election, with a minimum ten (10) seats guaranteed if the number of seats won is less than ten (10);

   (2) Parties, coalitions, citizens' initiatives and independent candidates having declared themselves representing the other Communities shall have the total number of seats won through the open election, with a minimum number of seats in the Assembly guaranteed as follows: the Roma community, one (1) seat; the Ashkali community, one (1) seat; the Egyptian community, one (1) seat; and one (1) additional seat will be awarded to either the Roma, the Ashkali or the Egyptian community with the highest overall votes; the Bosnian community, three (3) seats; the Turkish community, two
   (2) seats; and the Gorani community, one (1) seat if the number of seats won by each community is less than the number guaranteed.

Article 65   [Competencies of the Assembly]

The Assembly of the Republic of Kosovo:

   (1)   adopts laws, resolutions and other general acts;

   (2)   decides to amend the Constitution by two thirds (2/3) of all its deputies including two thirds (2/3) of all deputies holding seats reserved and guaranteed for representatives of communities that are not in the majority in Kosovo;

   (3)   announces referenda in accordance with the law;

   (4)   ratifies international treaties;

(5)   approves the budget of the Republic of Kosovo;

(6)   elects and dismisses the President and Deputy Presidents of the Assembly;

(7)   elects and may dismiss the President of the Republic of Kosovo in accordance with this Constitution;

(8)   elects the Government and expresses no confidence in it;

(9)   oversees the work of the Government and other public institutions that report to the Assembly in accordance with the Constitution and the law;

(10)   elects members of the Kosovo Judicial Council and the Kosovo Prosecutorial Council in accordance with this Constitution;

(11)   proposes the judges for the Constitutional Court;

(12)   oversees foreign and security policies;

(13)   gives consent to the President's decree announcing a State of Emergency;

(14)   decides in regard to general interest issues as set forth by law.

Article 66   [Election and Mandate]

1. The Assembly of Kosovo shall be elected for a mandate of four (4) years, starting from the day of the constitutive session, which shall be held within thirty (30) days from the official announcement of the election results.

2. Regular elections for the Assembly shall be held no later than thirty (30) days before the end of the mandate or, when the Assembly has been dissolved, no later than forty-five (45) days after the dissolution.

3. The President of the Republic of Kosovo shall convene the constitutive session of the Assembly. If the President of the Republic of Kosovo is unable to convene the initial session, the Assembly shall be convened without the President's participation.

4. The Mandate of the Assembly of Kosovo may be extended only in a State of Emergency for emergency defense measures or for danger to the Constitutional order or to public safety of the Republic of Kosovo and only for as long as the State of Emergency continues as regulated by this Constitution.

5. The election conditions, constituencies and procedures are determined by law.

Article 67   [Election of the President and Deputy Presidents]

1. The Assembly of Kosovo elects the President of the Assembly and five (5) Deputy Presidents from among its deputies.

2. The President of the Assembly is proposed by the largest parliamentary group and is elected by a majority vote of all deputies of the Assembly.

3. Three (3) Deputy Presidents proposed by the three largest parliamentary groups are elected by a majority vote of all deputies of the Assembly.

4. Two (2) Deputy Presidents represent non-majority communities in the Assembly and are elected by a majority vote of all deputies of the Assembly. One (1) Deputy President shall belong to the deputies of the Assembly holding seats reserved or guaranteed for the Serb community, and one (1) Deputy shall belong to deputies of the Assembly holding seats reserved or guaranteed for other communities that are not in the majority.

5. The President and Deputy Presidents of the Assembly are dismissed by a vote of two thirds (2/3) of all deputies of the Assembly.

6. The President and the Deputy Presidents form the Presidency of the Assembly. The Presidency is responsible for the administrative operation of the Assembly as provided in the Rules of Procedure of the Assembly.

7. The President of the Assembly:

   (1) represents the Assembly;

   (2) sets the agenda, convenes and chairs the sessions;

   (3) signs acts adopted by the Assembly;

   (4) exercises other functions in accordance with this Constitution and the Rules of Procedure of the Assembly.

8. When the President of the Assembly is absent or is unable to exercise the function, one of the Deputy Presidents will serve as President of the Assembly.

Article 68   [Sessions]

1. Meetings of the Assembly of Kosovo are public.

2. Meetings of the Assembly of Kosovo may be closed upon the request of the President of the Republic of Kosovo, the Prime Minister or one third (1/3) of the deputies of the Assembly as set forth by the Rules of Procedure of the Assembly. The decision shall be made in an open and transparent manner and must be adopted by two thirds (2/3) vote of the deputies of Assembly present and voting.

Article 69   [Schedule of Sessions and Quorum]

1. The Assembly of Kosovo conducts its annual work in two sessions.

2. The Spring Session begins on the third Monday of January and the Autumn session begins on the second Monday of September.

3. The Assembly of Kosovo has its quorum when more than one half (1/2) of all Assembly deputies are present.

4. The Assembly of Kosovo convenes an extraordinary meeting upon the request of the President of the Republic of Kosovo, the Prime Minister or one third (1/3) of the deputies.

Article 70 [Mandate of the Deputies]

1. Deputies of the Assembly are representatives of the people and are not bound by any obligatory mandate.

2. The mandate of each deputy of the Assembly of Kosovo begins on the day of the certification of the election results.

3. The mandate of a deputy of the Assembly comes to an end or becomes invalid when:

    (1) the deputy does not take the oath;

    (2) the deputy resigns;

    (3) the deputy becomes a member of the Government of Kosovo;

    (4) the mandate of the Assembly comes to an end;

    (5) the deputy is absent from the Assembly for more than six (6) consecutive months. In special cases, the Assembly of Kosovo can decide otherwise;

    (6) the deputy is convicted and sentenced to one or more years imprisonment by a final court decision of committing a crime;

    (7) the deputy dies.

4. Vacancies in the Assembly will be filled immediately in a manner consistent with this Constitution and as provided by law.

Article 71 [Qualification and Gender Equality]

1. Every citizen of the Republic of Kosovo who is eighteen (18) years or older and meets the legal criteria is eligible to become a candidate for the Assembly.

2. The composition of the Assembly of Kosovo shall respect internationally recognized principles of gender equality.

Article 72   [Incompatibility]

A member of the Assembly of Kosovo shall neither keep any executive post in the public administration or in any publicly owned enterprise nor exercise any other executive function as provided by law.

Article 73   [Ineligibility]

1. The following cannot be candidates or be elected as deputies of the Assembly without prior resignation from their duty:

    (1) judges and prosecutors;

    (2) members of the Kosovo Security Force;

    (3) members of the Kosovo Police;

    (4) members of the Customs Service of Kosovo;

    (5) members of the Kosovo Intelligence Agency;

    (6) heads of independent agencies;

    (7) diplomatic representatives;

    (8) chairpersons and members of the Central Election Commission.

2. Persons deprived of legal capacity by a final court decision are not eligible to become candidates for deputies of the Assembly.

3. Mayors and other officials holding executive responsibilities at the municipal level of municipalities cannot be elected as deputies of the Assembly without prior resignation from their duty.

Article 74   [Exercise of Function]

Deputies of the Assembly of Kosovo shall exercise their function in best interest of the Republic of Kosovo and pursuant to the Constitution, Laws and Rules of Procedure of the Assembly.

Article 75   [Immunity]

1. Deputies of the Assembly shall be immune from prosecution, civil lawsuit and dismissal for actions or decisions that are within the scope of their responsibilities as deputies of the Assembly. The immunity shall not prevent the criminal prosecution of deputies of the Assembly for actions taken outside of the scope of their responsibilities as deputies of the Assembly.

2. A member of the Assembly shall not be arrested or otherwise detained while performing her/his duties as a member of the Assembly without the consent of the majority of all deputies of the Assembly.

Article 76 [Rules of Procedure]

The Rules of Procedure of the Assembly are adopted by two thirds (2/3) vote of all its deputies and shall determine the internal organization and method of work for the Assembly.

Article 77 [Committees]

1. The Assembly of Kosovo appoints permanent committees, operational committees and ad hoc committees reflecting the political composition of the Assembly.

2. On the request of one third (1/3) of all of the deputies, the Assembly appoints committees for specific matters, including investigative matters.

3. At least one vice chair of each parliamentary committee shall be from the deputies of a Community different from the Community of the chair.

4. Competencies and procedures of the committees are defined in the Rules of Procedure of the Assembly.

Article 78 [Committee on Rights and Interests of Communities]

1. The Committee on Rights and Interests of Communities is a permanent committee of the Assembly. This committee is composed of one third (1/3) of members who represent the group of deputies of the Assembly holding seats reserved or guaranteed for the Serbian Community, one third (1/3) of members who represent the group of deputies of the Assembly holding seats reserved or guaranteed for other communities that are not in the majority and one third (1/3) of members from the majority community represented in the Assembly.

2. At the request of any member of the Presidency of the Assembly, any proposed law shall be submitted to the Committee on Rights and Interests of Communities. The Committee, by a majority vote of its members, shall decide whether to make recommendations regarding the proposed law within two weeks.

3. To ensure that community rights and interests are adequately addressed, the Committee may submit recommendations to another relevant committee or to the Assembly.

4. The Committee may, on its own initiative, propose laws and such other measures within the responsibilities of the Assembly as it deems appropriate to address the concerns of Communities. Members may issue individual opinions.

5. A matter may be referred to the Committee for an advisory opinion by the Presidency of the Assembly, another committee or a group composed of at least ten (10) deputies of the Assembly.

Article 79 [Legislative Initiative]

The initiative to propose laws may be taken by the President of the Republic of Kosovo from his/her scope of authority, the Government, deputies of the Assembly or at least ten thousand citizens as provided by law.

Article 80 [Adoption of Laws]

1. Laws, decisions and other acts are adopted by the Assembly by a majority vote of deputies present and voting, except when otherwise provided by the Constitution.

2. Laws adopted by the Assembly are signed by the President of the Assembly of Kosovo and promulgated by the President of the Republic of Kosovo upon her/his signature within eight (8) days from receipt.

3. If the President of the Republic of Kosovo returns a law to the Assembly, he/she should state the reasons of return. The President of the Republic of Kosovo may exercise this right of return only once per law.

4. The Assembly decides to adopt a law returned by the President of the Republic of Kosovo by a majority vote of all its deputies and such a law shall be considered promulgated.

5. If the President of the Republic of Kosovo does not make any decision for the promulgation or return of a law within eight (8) days from its receipt, such a law shall be considered promulgated without her/his signature and shall be published in the Official Gazette.

6. A law enters into force fifteen (15) days after its publication in the Official Gazette of the Republic of Kosovo, except when otherwise specified by the law itself.

Article 81 [Legislation of Vital Interest]

1. The following laws shall require for their adoption, amendment or repeal both the majority of the Assembly deputies present and voting and the majority of the Assembly deputies present and voting holding seats reserved or guaranteed for representatives of Communities that are not in the majority:

   (1) Laws changing municipal boundaries, establishing or abolishing municipalities, defining the scope of powers of municipalities and their participation in inter-municipal and cross-border relations;

   (2) Laws implementing the rights of Communities and their members, other than those set forth in the Constitution;

   (3) Laws on the use of language;

   (4) Laws on local elections;

(5) Laws on protection of cultural heritage;

(6) Laws on religious freedom or on agreements with religious communities;

(7) Laws on education;

(8) Laws on the use of symbols, including Community symbols and on public holidays.

2. None of the laws of vital interest may be submitted to a referendum.

Article 82 [Dissolution of the Assembly]

1. The Assembly shall be dissolved in the following cases:

(1) if the government cannot be established within sixty (60) days from the date when the President of the Republic of Kosovo appoints the candidate for Prime Minister;

(2) if two thirds (2/3) of all deputies vote in favor of dissolution, the Assembly shall be dissolved by a decree of the President of the Republic of Kosovo;

(3) if the President of the Republic of Kosovo is not elected within sixty (60) days from the date of the beginning of the president's election procedure.

2. The Assembly may be dissolved by the President of the Republic of Kosovo following a successful vote of no confidence against the Government.

Chapter V President of the Republic of Kosovo

Article 83   [Status of the President]

The President is the head of state and represents the unity of the people of the Republic of Kosovo.

Article 84   [Competencies of the President]

The President of the Republic of Kosovo:

(1)   represents the Republic of Kosovo, internally and externally;

(2)   guarantees the constitutional functioning of the institutions set forth by this Constitution;

(3)   announces elections for the Assembly of Kosovo and convenes its first meeting;

(4)   issues decrees in accordance with this Constitution;

(5)   promulgates laws approved by the Assembly of Kosovo;

(6)   has the right to return adopted laws for re-consideration, when he/she considers them to be harmful to the legitimate interests of the Republic of Kosovo or one or more Communities. This right can be exercised only once per law;

(7)   signs international agreements in accordance with this Constitution ;

(8)   proposes amendments to this Constitution;

(9)   may refer constitutional questions to the Constitutional Court.

(10)   leads the foreign policy of the country;

(11)   receives credentials of heads of diplomatic missions accredited to the Republic of Kosovo;

(12)   is the Commander-in-Chief of the Kosovo Security Force;

(13)   leads the Consultative Council for Communities;

(14)   appoints the candidate for Prime Minister for the establishment of the Government after proposal by the political party or coalition holding the majority in the Assembly;

(15)   appoints and dismisses the President of the Supreme Court of the Republic of Kosovo upon the proposal of the Kosovo Judicial Council;

(16) appoints and dismisses judges of the Republic of Kosovo upon the proposal of the Kosovo Judicial Council;

(17) appoints and dismisses the Chief Prosecutor of the Republic of Kosovo upon the proposal of the Kosovo Prosecutorial Council;

(18) appoints and dismisses prosecutors of the Republic of Kosovo upon the proposal of the Kosovo Prosecutorial Council;

(19) appoints judges to the Constitutional Court upon the proposal of the Assembly;

(20) appoints the Commander of the Kosovo Security Force upon recommendation of the Government;

(21) with the Prime Minister, jointly appoints the Director, Deputy Director and Inspector General of the Kosovo Intelligence Agency;

(22) decides to declare a State of Emergency in consultation with the Prime Minister;

(23) may request meetings of the Kosovo Security Council and chairs them during a State of Emergency;

(24) decides on the establishment of diplomatic and consular missions of the Republic of Kosovo in consultation with the Prime Minister;

(25) appoints and dismisses heads of diplomatic missions of the Republic of Kosovo upon the proposal of the Government;

(26) appoints the Chair of the Central Election Commission;

(27) appoints the Governor of the Central Bank of the Republic of Kosovo who will also act as its Managing Director, and appoints the other members of the Bank's Board;

(28) grants medals, titles of gratitude, and awards in accordance with the law;

(29) grants individual pardons in accordance with the law;

(30) addresses the Assembly of Kosovo at least once a year in regard to her/his scope of authority.

Article 85   [Qualification for Election of the President]

Every citizen of the Republic of Kosovo who is thirty five (35) years old or older may be elected President of the Republic of Kosovo.

Article 86   [Election of the President]

1. The President of the Republic of Kosovo shall be elected by the Assembly in secret ballot.

2. The election of the President of the Republic of Kosovo shall take place no later than thirty (30) days before the end of the current president's term of office.

3. Every eligible citizen of the Republic of Kosovo may be nominated as a candidate for President of the Republic of Kosovo, provided he/she presents the signatures of at least thirty (30) deputies of the Assembly of Kosovo. Deputies of the Assembly can only sign for one candidate for the President of the Republic.

4. The President of the Republic of Kosovo shall be elected by a two thirds (2/3) majority of all deputies of the Assembly.

5. If a two thirds (2/3) majority is not reached by any candidate in the first two ballots, a third ballot takes place between the two candidates who received the highest number of votes in the second ballot, and the candidate who receives the majority of all deputies of the Assembly shall be elected as President of the Republic of Kosovo.

6. If none of the candidates is elected as President of the Republic of Kosovo in the third ballot, the Assembly shall dissolve and new elections shall take place within forty five (45) days.

Article 87   [Mandate and Oath]

1. The President of the Republic of Kosovo begins her/his term of office after taking the oath before the Assembly of Kosovo. The text of the Oath will be provided by law.

2. The President's term of office is five (5) years.

3. Upon completion of his/her first term of office, the President of the Republic of Kosovo may be re-elected only once.

Article 88   [Incompatibility]

1. The President shall not exercise any other public function.

2. After election, the President cannot exercise any political party functions.

Article 89   [Immunity]

The President of the Republic of Kosovo shall be immune from prosecution, civil lawsuit and dismissal for actions or decisions that are within the scope of responsibilities of the President of the Republic of Kosovo.

Article 90   [Temporary Absence of the President]

1. If the President of the Republic of Kosovo is temporarily unable to fulfill her/his responsibilities, he/she may voluntarily transfer the duties of the position to the President

of the Assembly who shall then serve as Acting President of the Republic of Kosovo. The President's order of transfer shall state in particular the reason for the transfer and the duration of the transfer if known. The President of the Republic of Kosovo shall resume exercise of the duties of the position when she/he is able to do so and the President of the Assembly shall relinquish the position as Acting President.

2. When there is no voluntary transfer of power, the Assembly of the Republic of Kosovo determines by two thirds (2/3) vote of all deputies, after consultation with the medical consultants team, that the President of the Republic of Kosovo is temporarily unable to fulfill his/her responsibilities. The President of the Assembly shall serve as Acting President until the President of the Republic of Kosovo is able to resume carrying out her/his duties as President.

3. The position of Acting President of the Republic of Kosovo may not be exercised for a period longer than six (6) months.

Article 91   [Dismissal of the President]

1. The President of the Republic of Kosovo may be dismissed by the Assembly if he/she has been convicted of a serious crime or if she/he is unable to exercise the responsibilities of office due to serious illness or if the Constitutional Court has determined that he/she has committed a serious violation of the Constitution.

2. The procedure for dismissal of the President of the Republic of Kosovo may be initiated by one third (1/3) of the deputies of the Assembly who shall sign a petition explaining the reasons for dismissal. If the petition alleges serious illness, the Assembly shall consult the medical consultants team on the status of the President's health. If the petition alleges serious violation of the Constitution, the petition shall be immediately submitted to the Constitutional Court, which shall decide the matter within seven (7) days from the receipt of the petition.

3. If the President of the Republic of Kosovo has been convicted of a serious crime or if the Assembly in compliance with this article determines that the President is unable to exercise her/his responsibilities due to serious illness, or if the Constitutional Court has determined that he/she has seriously violated the Constitution, the Assembly may dismiss the President by two thirds (2/3) vote of all its deputies.

Chapter VI   Government of the Republic of Kosovo

Article 92   [General Principles]

1. The Government consists of the Prime Minister, deputy prime minister(s) and ministers.

2. The Government of Kosovo exercises the executive power in compliance with the Constitution and the law.

3. The Government implements laws and other acts adopted by the Assembly of Kosovo and exercises other activities within the scope of responsibilities set forth by the Constitution and the law.

4. The Government makes decisions in accordance with this Constitution and the laws, proposes draft laws, proposes amendments to existing laws or other acts and may give its opinion on draft laws that are not proposed by it.

Article 93   [Competencies of the Government]

The Government has the following competencies:

(1)   proposes and implements the internal and foreign policies of the country;

(2)   promotes the economic development of the country;

(3)   proposes draft laws and other acts to the Assembly;

(4)   makes decisions and issues legal acts or regulations necessary for the implementation of laws;

(5)   proposes the budget of the Republic of Kosovo;

(6)   guides and oversees the work of administration bodies;

(7)   guides the activities and the development of public services;

(8)   proposes to the President of the Republic of Kosovo the appointment and dismissal of the heads of diplomatic missions of the Republic of Kosovo;

(9)   proposes amendments to the Constitution;

(10)   may refer Constitutional questions to the Constitutional Court;

(11)   exercises other executive functions not assigned to other central or local level bodies.

Article 94 [Competencies of the Prime Minister]

The Prime Minister has the following competencies:

(1)   represents and leads the Government;

(2)   ensures that all Ministries act in accordance with government policies;

(3)   ensures the implementation of laws and policies determined by the Government;

(4)   may change members of the Government without the consent of the Assembly;

(5)   chairs the Kosovo Security Council;

(6)   appoints the Kosovo Police General Director;

(7)   consults with the President of the Republic of Kosovo on matters of intelligence;

(8)   in cooperation with the President, jointly appoints the Director, Deputy Director and Inspector General of the Kosovo Intelligence Agency;

(9)   consults with the President on the implementation of the foreign policy of the country;

(10)   performs other duties as set forth by the Constitution and the law.

Article 95 [Election of the Government]

1. After elections, the President of the Republic of Kosovo proposes to the Assembly a candidate for Prime Minister, in consultation with the political party or coalition that has won the majority in the Assembly necessary to establish the Government.

2. The candidate for Prime Minister, not later than fifteen (15) days from appointment, presents the composition of the Government to the Assembly and asks for Assembly approval.

3. The Government is considered elected when it receives the majority vote of all deputies of the Assembly of Kosovo.

4. If the proposed composition of the Government does not receive the necessary majority of votes, the President of the Republic of Kosovo appoints another candidate with the same procedure within ten (10) days. If the Government is not elected for the second time, the President of the Republic of Kosovo announces elections, which shall be held not later than forty (40) days from the date of announcement.

5. If the Prime Minister resigns or for any other reason the post becomes vacant, the Government ceases and the President of the Republic of Kosovo appoints a new candidate in consultation with the majority party or coalition that has won the majority in the Assembly to establish the Government.

6. After being elected, members of the Government shall take an Oath before the Assembly. The text of the Oath will be provided by law.

Article 96 [Ministries and Representation of Communities]

1. Ministries and other executive bodies are established as necessary to perform functions within the powers of the Government.

2. The number of members of Government is determined by an internal act of the Government.

3. There shall be at least one (1) Minister from the Kosovo Serb Community and one (1) Minister from another Kosovo non-majority Community. If there are more than twelve (12) Ministers, the Government shall have a third Minister representing a Kosovo non-majority Community.

4. There shall be at least two (2) Deputy Ministers from the Kosovo Serb Community and two (2) Deputy Ministers from other Kosovo non-majority Communities. If there are more than twelve (12) Ministers, the Government shall have a third Deputy Minister representing the Kosovo Serb Community and a third Deputy Minister representing another Kosovo non-majority Community.

5. The selection of these Ministers and Deputy Ministers shall be determined after consultations with parties, coalitions or groups representing Communities that are not in the majority in Kosovo. If appointed from outside the membership of the Kosovo Assembly, these Ministers and Deputy Ministers shall require the formal endorsement of the majority of Assembly deputies belonging to parties, coalitions, citizens' initiatives and independent candidates having declared themselves to represent the Community concerned.

6. The Prime Minister, Deputy Prime Minister(s) and Ministers of the Government may be elected from the deputies of the Assembly of Kosovo or may be qualified people who are not deputies of the Assembly.

7. The incompatibilities of the members of the Government as to their functions shall be regulated by law.

Article 97 [Responsibilities]

1. The Government is accountable to the Assembly of Kosovo regarding its work.

2. The Prime Minister, deputy prime minister(s) and ministers are jointly accountable for the decisions made by the Government and individually accountable for decisions made in their fields of responsibility.

Article 98   [Immunity]

Members of the Government shall be immune from prosecution, civil lawsuit and dismissal for actions or decisions that are within the scope of their responsibilities as members of the Government.

Article 99   [Procedures]

The methods of work and decision making procedures of the Government shall be regulated by law and regulations.

Article 100   [Motion of No Confidence]

1. A motion of no confidence may be presented against the Government on the proposal of one third (1/3) of all the deputies of the Assembly.

2. A vote of confidence for the Government may be requested by the Prime Minister.

3. The motion of no confidence shall be placed on the Assembly agenda no later than five (5) days nor earlier than two (2) days from the date it was presented.

4. The motion of no confidence is considered accepted when adopted by a majority vote of all deputies of the Assembly of Kosovo.

5. If a motion of no confidence fails, a subsequent motion for no confidence may not be raised during the next ninety (90) days.

6. If a motion of no confidence against the Government prevails, the Government is considered dismissed.

Article 101   [Civil Service]

1. The composition of the civil service shall reflect the diversity of the people of Kosovo and take into account internationally recognized principles of gender equality.

2. An independent oversight board for civil service shall ensure the respect of the rules and principles governing the civil service, and shall itself reflect the diversity of the people of the Republic of Kosovo.

Chapter VII   Justice System

Article 102   [General Principles of the Judicial System]

1. Judicial power in the Republic of Kosovo is exercised by the courts.

2. The judicial power is unique, independent, fair, apolitical and impartial and ensures equal access to the courts.

3. Courts shall adjudicate based on the Constitution and the law.

4. Judges shall be independent and impartial in exercising their functions.

5. The right to appeal a judicial decision is guaranteed unless otherwise provided by law. The right to extraordinary legal remedies is regulated by law. The law may allow the right to refer a case directly to the Supreme Court, in which case there would be no right of appeal.

Article 103   [Organization and Jurisdiction of Courts]

1. Organization, functioning and jurisdiction of the Supreme Court and other courts shall be regulated by law.

2. The Supreme Court of Kosovo is the highest judicial authority.

3. At least fifteen percent (15%) of the judges of the Supreme Court, but not fewer than three (3) judges, shall be from Communities that are not in the majority in Kosovo.

4. The President of the Supreme Court of Kosovo shall be appointed and dismissed by the President of the Republic of Kosovo from among the judges of the Supreme Court for a non-renewable term of seven (7) years upon proposal by the Kosovo Judicial Council for the appointment or dismissal.

5. Presidents of all other courts shall be appointed in the manner provided by law.

6. At least fifteen percent (15%) of the judges from any other court established with appeal jurisdiction, but not fewer than two (2) judges, shall be from Communities that are not in the majority in Kosovo.

7. Specialized courts may be established by law when necessary, but no extraordinary court may ever be created.

Article 104   [Appointment and Removal of Judges]

1. The President of the Republic of Kosovo shall appoint, reappoint and dismiss judges upon the proposal of the Kosovo Judicial Council.

2. The composition of the judiciary shall reflect the ethnic diversity of Kosovo and internationally recognized principles of gender equality.

3. The composition of the courts shall reflect the ethnic composition of the territorial jurisdiction of the respective court. Before making a proposal for appointment or reappointment, the Kosovo Judicial Council consults with the respective court.

4. Judges may be removed from office upon conviction of a serious criminal offense or for serious neglect of duties.

5. A judge has the right to directly appeal a decision of dismissal to the Kosovo Supreme Court.

6. Judges may not be transferred against their will unless otherwise provided by law for the efficient operation of the judiciary or disciplinary measures.

Article 105   [Mandate and Reappointment]

1. The initial mandate for judges shall be three years. The reappointment mandate is permanent until the retirement age as determined by law or unless removed in accordance with law.

2. The criteria and procedures to reappoint a judge shall be determined by the Kosovo Judicial Council and they may be different in degree from the criteria used for the removal of judges.

Article 106   [Incompatibility]

1. A judge may not perform any function in any state institution outside of the judiciary, become involved in any political activity, or be involved in any other activity prohibited by law.

2. Judges are not permitted to assume any responsibilities or take on any functions that would in any way be inconsistent with the principles of independence and impartiality of the role of a judge.

Article 107   [Immunity]

1. Judges, including lay-judges, shall be immune from prosecution, civil lawsuit and dismissal for actions taken, decisions made or opinions expressed that are within the scope of their responsibilities as judges.

2. Judges, including lay-judges, shall not enjoy immunity and may be removed from office if they have committed an intentional violation of the law.

3. When a judge is indicted or arrested, notice must be given to the Kosovo Judicial Council without delay.

Article 108 [Kosovo Judicial Council]

1. The Kosovo Judicial Council shall ensure the independence and impartiality of the judicial system.

2. The Kosovo Judicial Council is a fully independent institution in the performance of its functions. The Kosovo Judicial Council shall ensure that the Kosovo courts are independent, professional and impartial and fully reflect the multi-ethnic nature of Kosovo and follow the principles of gender equality. The Kosovo Judicial Council shall give preference in the appointment of judges to members of Communities that are underrepresented in the judiciary as provided by law.

3. The Kosovo Judicial Council is responsible for recruiting and proposing candidates for appointment and reappointment to judicial office. The Kosovo Judicial Council is also responsible for transfer and disciplinary proceedings of judges.

4. Proposals for appointments of judges must be made on the basis of an open appointment process, on the basis of the merit of the candidates, and the proposals shall reflect principles of gender equality and the ethnic composition of the territorial jurisdiction of the respective court. All candidates must fulfill the selection criteria provided by law.

5. The Kosovo Judicial Council is responsible for conducting judicial inspections, judicial administration, developing court rules in accordance with the law, hiring and supervising court administrators, developing and overseeing the budget of the judiciary, determining the number of judges in each jurisdiction and making recommendations for the establishment of new courts. New courts shall be established according to law.

6. The Kosovo Judicial Council shall be composed of thirteen (13) members, all of whom shall possess relevant professional qualifications and expertise. Members shall be elected for a term of five (5) years and shall be chosen in the following manner:

   (1) five (5) members shall be judges elected by the members of the judiciary;

   (2) four (4) members shall be elected by deputies of the Assembly holding seats attributed during the general distribution of seats; at least two (2) of the four (4) must be judges and one (1) must be a member of the Kosovo Chamber of Advocates;

   (3) two (2) members shall be elected by the deputies of the Assembly holding reserved or guaranteed seats for the Kosovo Serb community and at least one of the two must be a judge;

   (4) two (2) members shall be elected by the deputies of the Assembly holding reserved or guaranteed seats for other Communities and at least one of the two must be a judge.

   (5) Incompatibilities with membership on the Kosovo Judicial Council shall be regulated by law.

7. The Kosovo Judicial Council elects from its members a Chair and Vice Chair each for a term of three (3) years. Election to these offices does not extend the mandate of the members of the Kosovo Judicial Council.

8. The Chair of the Kosovo Judicial Council addresses the Assembly of the Republic of Kosovo at least once a year regarding the Judicial System.

9. Candidates for judicial positions that are reserved for members of Communities that are not in the majority in Kosovo may only be recommended for appointment by the majority of members of the Council elected by Assembly deputies holding seats reserved or guaranteed for members of communities that are not in the majority in Kosovo. If this group of Council members fails to recommend a candidate for a judicial position in two consecutive sessions of the Council, any Council member may recommend a candidate for that position.

10. Candidates for judicial positions within basic courts, the jurisdiction of which exclusively includes the territory of one or more municipalities in which the majority of the population belongs to the Kosovo Serb community, may only be recommended for appointment by the two members of the Council elected by Assembly deputies holding seats reserved or guaranteed for the Serb Community in the Republic of Kosovo acting jointly and unanimously. If these two (2) members fail to recommend a judicial candidate for two consecutive sessions of the Kosovo Judicial Council, any Kosovo Judicial Council member may recommend a candidate for that position.

Article 109   [State Prosecutor]

1. The State Prosecutor is an independent institution with authority and responsibility for the prosecution of persons charged with committing criminal acts and other acts specified by law.

2. The State Prosecutor is an impartial institution and acts in accordance with the Constitution and the law.

3. The organization, competencies and duties of the State Prosecutor shall be defined by law.

4. The State Prosecutor shall reflect the multiethnic composition of the Republic of Kosovo and shall respect the principles of gender equality.

5. The mandate for prosecutors shall be three years. The reappointment mandate is permanent until the retirement age as determined by law or unless removed in accordance with law.

6. Prosecutors may be removed from office upon conviction of a serious criminal offense or for serious neglect of duties.

7. The Chief State Prosecutor shall be appointed and dismissed by the President of the Republic of Kosovo upon the proposal of the Kosovo Prosecutorial Council. The mandate of the Chief State Prosecutor is seven (7) years, without the possibility of reappointment.

Article 110   [Kosovo Prosecutorial Council]

1. The Kosovo Prosecutorial Council is a fully independent institution in the performance of its functions in accordance with law. The Kosovo Prosecutorial Council shall ensure that all persons have equal access to justice. The Kosovo Prosecutorial Council shall ensure that the State Prosecutor is independent, professional and impartial and reflects the multi-ethnic nature of Kosovo and the principles of gender equality.

2. The Kosovo Prosecutorial Council shall recruit, propose, promote, transfer, reappoint and discipline prosecutors in a manner provided by law. The Council shall give preference for appointment as prosecutors to members of underrepresented Communities as provided by law. All candidates shall fulfill the selection criteria as provided by law.

3. Proposals for appointments of prosecutors must be made on the basis of an open appointment process, on the basis of the merit of the candidates, and the proposals shall reflect principles of gender equality and the ethnic composition of the relevant territorial jurisdiction.

4. The composition of Kosovo Prosecutorial Council, as well as provisions regarding appointment, removal, term of office, organizational structure and rules of procedure, shall be determined by law.

Article 111   [Advocacy]

1. Advocacy is an independent profession, which shall provide services in the manner provided by law.

2. The manners by which the right of exercising the profession of the advocate is obtained and lost shall be determined by law.

Chapter VIII   Constitutional Court

Article 112   [General Principles]

1. The Constitutional Court is the final authority for the interpretation of the Constitution and the compliance of laws with the Constitution.

2. The Constitutional Court is fully independent in the performance of its responsibilities.

Article 113   [Jurisdiction and Authorized Parties]

1. The Constitutional Court decides only on matters referred to the court in a legal manner by authorized parties.

2. The Assembly of Kosovo, the President of the Republic of Kosovo, the Government, and the Ombudsperson are authorized to refer the following matters to the Constitutional Court:

   (1) the question of the compatibility with the Constitution of laws, of decrees of the President or Prime Minister, and of regulations of the Government;

   (2) the compatibility with the Constitution of municipal statutes.

3. The Assembly of Kosovo, the President of the Republic of Kosovo and the Government are authorized to refer the following matters to the Constitutional Court:

   (1) conflict among constitutional competencies of the Assembly of Kosovo, the President of the Republic of Kosovo and the Government of Kosovo;

   (2) compatibility with the Constitution of a proposed referendum;

   (3) compatibility with the Constitution of the declaration of a State of Emergency and the actions undertaken during the State of Emergency;

   (4) compatibility of a proposed constitutional amendment with binding international agreements ratified under this Constitution and the review of the constitutionality of the procedure followed;

   (5) questions whether violations of the Constitution occurred during the election of the Assembly.

4. A municipality may contest the constitutionality of laws or acts of the Government infringing upon their responsibilities or diminishing their revenues when municipalities are affected by such law or act.

5. Ten (10) or more deputies of the Assembly of Kosovo, within eight (8) days from the date of adoption, have the right to contest the constitutionality of any law or decision adopted by the Assembly as regards its substance and the procedure followed.

6. Thirty (30) or more deputies of the Assembly are authorized to refer the question of whether the President of the Republic of Kosovo has committed a serious violation of the Constitution.

7. Individuals are authorized to refer violations by public authorities of their individual rights and freedoms guaranteed by the Constitution, but only after exhaustion of all legal remedies provided by law.

8. The courts have the right to refer questions of constitutional compatibility of a law to the Constitutional Court when it is raised in a judicial proceeding and the referring court is uncertain as to the compatibility of the contested law with the Constitution and provided that the referring court's decision on that case depends on the compatibility of the law at issue.

9. The President of the Assembly of Kosovo refers proposed Constitutional amendments before approval by the Assembly to confirm that the proposed amendment does not diminish the rights and freedoms guaranteed by Chapter II of the Constitution.

10. Additional jurisdiction may be determined by law.

Article 114 [Composition and Mandate of the Constitutional Court]

1. The Constitutional Court shall be composed of nine (9) judges who shall be distinguished jurists of the highest moral character, with not less than ten (10) years of relevant professional experience. Other relevant qualifications shall be provided by law. Principles of gender equality shall be respected.

2. Judges shall be appointed by the President of the Republic of Kosovo upon the proposal of the Assembly and shall serve for a non-renewable mandate of nine (9) years.

3. The decision to propose seven (7) judges requires a two thirds (2/3) majority of the deputies of the Assembly present and voting. The decision on the proposals of the other two (2) judges shall require the majority vote of the deputies of the Assembly present and voting, but only upon the consent of the majority of the deputies of the Assembly holding seats reserved or guaranteed for representatives of the Communities not in the majority in Kosovo.

4. If the mandate of a judge ends before the end of the regular mandate, the appointment of the replacement judge shall be made in compliance with this article for a full mandate without the right to re-appointment.

5. The President and Deputy President of the Constitutional Court shall be elected from the judges of the Constitutional Court by a secret ballot of the judges of the Court for a term of three (3) years. Election to these offices shall not extend the regular mandate of the judge.

Article 115   [Organization of the Constitutional Court]

1. The Constitutional Court shall determine its internal organization, rules of procedure, decision-making processes and other organizational issues pursuant to law.

2. The Constitutional Court shall publish an annual report.

Article 116   [Legal Effect of Decisions]

1. Decisions of the Constitutional Court are binding on the judiciary and all persons and institutions of the Republic of Kosovo.

2. While a proceeding is pending before the Constitutional Court, the Court may temporarily suspend the contested action or law until the Court renders a decision if the Court finds that application of the contested action or law would result in unrecoverable damages.

3. If not otherwise provided by the Constitutional Court decision, the repeal of the law or other act or action is effective on the day of the publication of the Court decision.

4. Decisions of the Constitutional Court are published in the Official Gazette.

Article 117   [Immunity]

Judges of the Constitutional Court shall be immune from prosecution, civil lawsuit and dismissal for actions taken, decisions made or opinions expressed that are within the scope of their responsibilities as Judges of the Constitutional Court.

Article 118   [Dismissal]

Judges of the Constitutional Court may be dismissed by the President of the Republic of Kosovo upon the proposal of two thirds (2/3) of the judges of the Constitutional Court only for the commission of a serious crime or for serious neglect of duties.

Chapter IX   Economic Relations

Article 119   [General Principles]

1. The Republic of Kosovo shall ensure a favorable legal environment for a market economy, freedom of economic activity and safeguards for private and public property.

2. The Republic of Kosovo shall ensure equal legal rights for all domestic and foreign investors and enterprises.

3. Actions limiting free competition through the establishment or abuse of a dominant position or practices restricting competition are prohibited, unless explicitly allowed by law.

4. The Republic of Kosovo promotes the welfare of all of its citizens by fostering sustainable economic development.

5. The Republic of Kosovo shall establish independent market regulators where the market alone cannot sufficiently protect the public interest.

6. A foreign investor is guaranteed the right to freely transfer profit and invested capital outside the country in accordance with the law.

7. Consumer protection is guaranteed in accordance with the law.

8. Every person is required to pay taxes and other contributions as provided by law.

9. The Republic of Kosovo shall exercise its ownership function over any enterprise it controls consistently with the public interest, with a view to maximizing the long-term value of the enterprise.

10. Public service obligation may be imposed on such enterprises in accordance with the law, which shall also provide for a fair compensation.

Article 120   [Public Finances]

1. Public expenditure and the collection of public revenue shall be based on the principles of accountability, effectiveness, efficiency and transparency.

2. The conduct of fiscal policy at all levels of government shall be compatible with the conditions for low-inflationary and sustainable economic growth and employment creation.

3. Public borrowing shall be regulated by law and shall be compatible with economic stability and fiscal sustainability.

Article 121 [Property]

1. Types of property shall be defined by law.

2. Foreign natural persons and foreign organizations may acquire ownership rights over immovable property in accordance with such reasonable conditions as may be established by law or international agreement.

3. Foreign natural persons and foreign organizations may, in accordance with such reasonable conditions as may be established by law, acquire concession rights and other rights to use and/or exploit publicly owned resources, including natural resources, and publicly owned infrastructure.

Article 122 [Use of Property and Natural Resources]

1. The people of the Republic of Kosovo may, in accordance with such reasonable conditions as may be established by law, enjoy the natural resources of the Republic of Kosovo, but they may not infringe on the obligations stemming from international agreements on economic cooperation.

2. Natural resources such as water, air space, mineral resources and other natural resources including land, flora and fauna, other parts of nature, immovable property and other goods of special cultural, historic, economic and ecologic importance, which have been determined by law to be of special interest to the Republic of Kosovo, shall enjoy special protection in accordance with law.

3. Limitations on owners' rights and other exploitation rights on goods of special interest to the Republic of Kosovo and the compensation for such limitations shall be provided by law.

Chapter X Local Government and Territorial Organization

Article 123   [General Principles]

1. The right to local self-government is guaranteed and is regulated by law.

2. Local self-government is exercised by representative bodies elected through general, equal, free, direct, and secret ballot elections.

3. The activity of local self-government bodies is based on this Constitution and the laws of the Republic of Kosovo and respects the European Charter of Local Self-Government. The Republic of Kosovo shall observe and implement the European Charter on Local Self Government to the same extent as that required of a signatory state.

4. Local self-government is based upon the principles of good governance, transparency, efficiency and effectiveness in providing public services having due regard for the specific needs and interests of the Communities not in the majority and their members.

Article 124   [Local Self-Government Organization and Operation]

1. The basic unit of local government in the Republic of Kosovo is the municipality. Municipalities enjoy a high degree of local self-governance and encourage and ensure the active participation of all citizens in the decision-making process of the municipal bodies.

2. Establishment of municipalities, municipal boundaries, competencies and method of organization and operation shall be regulated by law.

3. Municipalities have their own, extended and delegated competencies in accordance with the law. The state authority which delegates competencies shall cover the expenditures incurred for the exercise of delegation.

4. Municipalities have the right of inter-municipal cooperation and cross-border cooperation in accordance with the law.

5. Municipalities have the right to decide, collect and spend municipal revenues and receive appropriate funding from the central government in accordance with the law.

6. Municipalities are bound to respect the Constitution and laws and to apply court decisions.

7. The administrative review of acts of municipalities by the central authorities in the area of their own competencies shall be limited to ensuring compatibility with the Constitution of the Republic of Kosovo and the law.

Chapter XI   Security Sector

Article 125   [General Principles]

1. The Republic of Kosovo has authority over law enforcement, security, justice, public safety, intelligence, civil emergency response and border control within its territory.

2. Security institutions in the Republic of Kosovo shall protect public safety and the rights of all people in the Republic of Kosovo. The institutions shall operate in full transparency and in accordance with internationally recognized democratic standards and human rights. Security institutions shall reflect the ethnic diversity of the population of the Republic of Kosovo.

3. The Republic of Kosovo fully respects all applicable international agreements and the relevant international law and cooperates with the international security bodies and regional counterparts.

4. Civilian and democratic control over security institutions shall be guaranteed.

5. The Assembly of the Republic of Kosovo oversees the budget and policies of the security institutions as provided by law.

Article 126   [Kosovo Security Force]

1. The Kosovo Security Force shall serve as a national security force for the Republic of Kosovo and may send its members abroad in full conformity with its international responsibilities.

2. The Kosovo Security Force shall protect the people and Communities of the Republic of Kosovo based on the competencies provided by law.

3. The President of the Republic of Kosovo is the Commander-in-Chief of the Kosovo Security Force, which shall always be subject to control by democratically elected civilian authorities.

4. The Kosovo Security Force shall be professional, reflect ethnic diversity of the people of the Republic of Kosovo and shall be recruited from among the citizens of the Republic of Kosovo.

5. The Commander of the Kosovo Security Force shall be appointed by the President of the Republic of Kosovo upon the recommendation of the Government. Internal organization of the Kosovo Security Force shall be determined by law.

Article 127   [Kosovo Security Council]

1. The Security Council of the Republic of Kosovo in cooperation with the President of the Republic of Kosovo and the Government develops the security strategy for the Republic of

Kosovo. The Security Council of the Republic of Kosovo shall also have an advisory role on all matters relating to security in the Republic of Kosovo.

2. The Security Council of the Republic of Kosovo shall be chaired by the Prime Minister with the support of the Government, except during a State of Emergency as provided by this Constitution.

3. The President of the Republic of Kosovo may require meetings of the Security Council of the Republic of Kosovo and the Council is obliged to closely coordinate its work with the President. The Security Council of the Republic of Kosovo shall closely cooperate with international authorities.

4. Members of the Security Council of the Republic of Kosovo shall be appointed and dismissed in a manner provided for by law.

Article 128   [Kosovo Police]

1. The Police of the Republic of Kosovo shall be responsible for the preservation of public order and safety throughout the territory of the Republic of Kosovo.

2. The Police shall be professional and reflect the ethnic diversity of the population of the Republic of Kosovo.

3. The Prime Minister shall appoint the Police Director General of the Republic of Kosovo upon the recommendation of the Government and in accordance with law. Internal organization of the Kosovo Police shall be provided by law.

4. The Police of the Republic of Kosovo shall have a unified chain of command throughout the Republic of Kosovo with police stations corresponding to municipal boundaries. The Kosovo Police shall facilitate cooperation with municipal authorities and community leaders through the establishment of Local Councils as provided by law. Ethnic composition of the police within a municipality shall reflect the ethnic composition of the population within the respective municipality to the highest extent possible.

5. The Police of the Republic of Kosovo shall be responsible for border control in direct cooperation with local and international authorities.

Article 129   [Kosovo Intelligence Agency]

1. The Kosovo Intelligence Agency shall identify, investigate and monitor threats to security in the Republic of Kosovo.

2. The Kosovo Intelligence Agency shall be professional, politically impartial, multi-ethnic and shall be subject to Assembly oversight in a manner provided by law.

3. The President of the Republic of Kosovo and the Prime Minister, upon consultation with the Government, shall jointly appoint the Director, Deputy Director and Inspector General of Kosovo Intelligence Agency. Qualifications and terms of office shall be determined by law.

4. The President of the Republic of Kosovo and the Prime Minister shall receive the same intelligence information.

Article 130   [Civilian Aviation Authority]

1. The Civilian Aviation Authority of the Republic of Kosovo shall regulate civilian aviation activities in the Republic of Kosovo and shall be a provider of air navigation services as provided by law.

2. The Civilian Aviation Authority shall fully cooperate with relevant international and local authorities as provided by law.

Article 131   [State of Emergency]

1. The President of the Republic of Kosovo may declare a State of Emergency when:

   (1) there is a need for emergency defense measures;

   (2) there is internal danger to the constitutional order or to public security; or

   (3) there is a natural disaster affecting all or part of the territory of the Republic of Kosovo.

2. During the State of Emergency, the Constitution of the Republic of Kosovo shall not be suspended. Limitations on the rights and freedoms guaranteed by the Constitution shall only be to the extent necessary, for the least amount of time and in full accordance with this Constitution. During the State of Emergency, the law on elections of the Assembly and Municipalities shall not be changed. Further principles for the actions of the public institutions during the State of Emergency shall be regulated by law, but shall not be inconsistent with this Article.

3. If there exists the need for emergency defense measures, the President of the Republic of Kosovo shall declare a State of Emergency upon consultation with the Prime Minister. In declaring the State of Emergency, the President of the Republic of Kosovo shall immediately issue a decree setting forth the nature of the threat and any limitations on rights and freedoms. Within forty eight (48) hours, the Assembly may provide its consent by two thirds (2/3) vote of the deputies present and voting. If consent is not provided, the President's decree shall have no force or effect.

4. If there exists a danger to the constitutional order and to the public safety in the Republic of Kosovo or there exists a natural disaster in all or part of the territory of the Republic of Kosovo, the President of the Republic of Kosovo may declare a State of Emergency upon consultation with the Prime Minister. In declaring the State of Emergency, the President of the Republic of Kosovo shall immediately issue a decree setting forth the nature of the emergency and any limitations on rights and freedoms. Within forty eight (48) hours, the Assembly may provide its consent by a majority vote of the deputies present and voting. If consent is not provided, the President's decree shall have no force or effect.

5. A State of Emergency shall last only as long as the danger continues and may last no longer than a period of sixty (60) days. With the consent of a majority vote of the deputies of the Assembly present and voting, the State of Emergency may be extended if necessary for successive periods of thirty (30) days up to a total of ninety (90) additional days.

6. The Assembly may place such limitations on the duration and extent of the State of Emergency as deemed necessary. When the President determines that the danger to the Republic of Kosovo is of an extraordinary nature, the Assembly may authorize an extension of the State of Emergency beyond the one hundred fifty (150) days, only if adopted by two thirds (2/3) vote of all deputies of the Assembly.

7. The President of the Republic of Kosovo may, upon consultation with the Government and the Assembly, order mobilization of the Kosovo Security Force to assist in the State of Emergency.

8. The Security Council of the Republic of Kosovo, only during the State of Emergency, shall exercise executive functions which shall be limited to those functions which specifically relate to the State of Emergency. In a State of Emergency the Security Council of the Republic of Kosovo shall be chaired by the President of the Republic of Kosovo, as provided by law. During the State of Emergency, the Security Council of the Republic of Kosovo shall closely cooperate with the Government, the Assembly and international authorities.

9. The law shall define the principles, areas and manner of compensation for any losses resulting from the limitations imposed during a State of Emergency.

Chapter XII   Independent Institutions

Article 132   [Role and Competencies of the Ombudsperson]

1. The Ombudsperson monitors, defends and protects the rights and freedoms of individuals from unlawful or improper acts or failures to act of public authorities.

2. The Ombudsperson independently exercises her/his duty and does not accept any instructions or intrusions from the organs, institutions or other authorities exercising state authority in the Republic of Kosovo.

3. Every organ, institution or other authority exercising legitimate power of the Republic of Kosovo is bound to respond to the requests of the Ombudsperson and shall submit all requested documentation and information in conformity with the law.

Article 133   [Office of Ombudsperson]

1. The Office of the Ombudsperson shall be an independent office and shall propose and administer its budget in a manner provided by law.

2. The Ombudsperson has one (1) or more deputies. Their number, method of selection and mandate are determined by the Law on Ombudsperson. At least one (1) Deputy Ombudsperson shall be a member of a Community not in the majority in Kosovo.

Article 134   [Qualification, Election and Dismissal of the Ombudsperson]

1. The Ombudsperson is elected by the Assembly of Kosovo by a majority of all its deputies for a non-renewable five (5) year term.

2. Any citizen of the Republic of Kosovo, who has a university degree, high moral and honest character, distinguished experience and knowledge in the area of human rights and freedoms, is eligible to be elected as Ombudsperson.

3. The Ombudsperson and Deputy Ombudspersons shall not be members of any political party, exercise any political, state or professional private activity, or participate in the management of civil, economic or trade organizations.

4. The Ombudsperson shall be immune from prosecution, civil lawsuit and dismissal for actions or decisions that are within the scope of responsibilities of the Ombudsperson.

5. The Ombudsperson may be dismissed only upon the request of more than one third (1/3) of all deputies of the Assembly and upon a vote of two thirds (2/3) majority of all its deputies.

Article 135 [Ombudsperson Reporting]

1. The Ombudsperson shall submit an annual report to the Assembly of the Republic of Kosovo.

2. Upon request of the Assembly, the Ombudsperson is required to submit interim or other reports to the Assembly. Upon the request of the Ombudsperson, the Assembly shall permit the Ombudsperson to be heard.

3. The Ombudsperson is eligible to make recommendations and propose actions when violations of human rights and freedoms by the public administration and other state authorities are observed.

4. The Ombudsperson may refer matters to the Constitutional Court in accordance with the provisions of this Constitution.

Article 136 [Auditor-General of Kosovo]

1. The Auditor-General of the Republic of Kosovo is the highest institution of economic and financial control.

2. Organization, operation and competencies of the Auditor-General of the Republic of Kosovo shall be determined by the Constitution and law.

3. The Auditor-General of the Republic of Kosovo is elected and dismissed by the Assembly by a majority vote of all its deputies on the proposal of the President of the Republic of Kosovo.

4. The Assembly decides on the dismissal of the Auditor-General of the Republic of Kosovo by a two thirds (2/3) majority of all its deputies upon the proposal of the President of the Republic of Kosovo or upon the proposal of one third (1/3) of all its deputies.

5. The mandate of the Auditor-General of the Republic of Kosovo is five (5) years with the possibility of re-election to only one additional mandate.

Article 137 [Competencies of the Auditor-General of Kosovo]

Auditor-General of the Republic of Kosovo audits:

(1) the economic activity of public institutions and other state legal persons;

(2) the use and safeguarding of public funds by central and local authorities;

(3) the economic activity of public enterprises and other legal persons in which the State has shares or the loans, credits and liabilities of which are guaranteed by the State.

Article 138   [Reports of the Auditor-General of Kosovo]

1. The Auditor-General of the Republic of Kosovo addresses the Assembly:

    (1) to report on the execution of the State budget;

    (2) to give an opinion on the report of the Government on its expenditures of the previous year before it is adopted by the Assembly;

    (3) to inform the Assembly on conclusions of audits when requested.

2. The Auditor-General of the Republic of Kosovo submits an annual report on the activities of the office to the Assembly.

Article 139   [Central Election Commission]

1. The Central Election Commission is a permanent body, which prepares, supervises, directs, and verifies all activities related to the process of elections and referenda and announces their results.

2. The Commission is composed of eleven (11) members.

3. The Chair of the Central Election Commission is appointed by the President of the Republic of Kosovo from among the judges of the Supreme Court and courts exercising appellate jurisdiction.

4. Six (6) members shall be appointed by the six largest parliamentary groups represented in the Assembly, which are not entitled to reserved seats. If fewer groups are represented in the Assembly, the largest group or groups may appoint additional members. One (1) member shall be appointed by the Assembly deputies holding seats reserved or guaranteed for the Kosovo Serb Community, and three (3) members shall be appointed by the Assembly deputies holding seats reserved or guaranteed for other Communities that are not in majority in Kosovo.

Article 140   [Central Bank of Kosovo]

1. The Central Bank of the Republic of Kosovo is an independent institution which reports to the Assembly of Kosovo.

2. The Central Bank of the Republic of Kosovo exercises its competencies and powers exclusively in accordance with this Constitution and other applicable legislative instruments.

3. The Governor of the Central Bank of the Republic of Kosovo will serve as the Chief Executive Officer.

4. The governance of the Central Bank of the Republic of Kosovo and the selection and nomination procedures of the Central Bank Board members shall be regulated by law, which shall ensure its independence and autonomy.

Article 141   [Independent Media Commission]

1. The Independent Media Commission is an independent body, which regulates the Range of Broadcasting Frequencies in the Republic of Kosovo, issues licenses to public and private broadcasters, establishes and implements broadcasting policies and exercises other competencies as set forth by law.

2. The members of the Independent Media Commission shall be elected in a transparent process in accordance with the law.

Article 142   [Independent Agencies]

1. Independent agencies of the Republic of Kosovo are institutions established by the Assembly based on the respective laws that regulate their establishment, operation and competencies. Independent agencies exercise their functions independently from any other body or authority in the Republic of Kosovo.

2. Independent agencies have their own budget that shall be administered independently in accordance with the law.

3. Every organ, institution or other entity exercising legal authority in the Republic of Kosovo is bound to cooperate with and respond to the requests of the independent agencies during the exercise of their legal competencies in a manner provided by law.

Chapter XIII   Final Provisions

Article 143   [Comprehensive Proposal for the Kosovo Status Settlement]

Notwithstanding any provision of this Constitution:

1. All authorities in the Republic of Kosovo shall abide by all of the Republic of Kosovo's obligations under the Comprehensive Proposal for the Kosovo Status Settlement dated 26 March 2007. They shall take all necessary actions for their implementation.

2. The provisions of the Comprehensive Proposal for the Kosovo Status Settlement dated 26 March 2007 shall take precedence over all other legal provisions in Kosovo.

3. The Constitution, laws and other legal acts of the Republic of Kosovo shall be interpreted in compliance with the Comprehensive Proposal for the Kosovo Status Settlement dated 26 March 2007. If there are inconsistencies between the provisions of this Constitution, laws or other legal acts of the Republic of Kosovo and the provisions of the said Settlement, the latter shall prevail.

Article 144   [Amendments]

1. The Government, the President or one fourth (1/4) of the deputies of the Assembly of Kosovo as set forth in the Rules of Procedure of the Assembly may propose changes and amendments to this Constitution.

2. Any amendment shall require for its adoption the approval of two thirds (2/3) of all deputies of the Assembly including two thirds (2/3) of all deputies of the Assembly holding reserved or guaranteed seats for representatives of communities that are not in the majority in the Republic of Kosovo.

3. Amendments to this Constitution may be adopted by the Assembly only after the President of the Assembly of Kosovo has referred the proposed amendment to the Constitutional Court for a prior assessment that the proposed amendment does not diminish any of the rights and freedoms set forth in Chapter II of this Constitution.

4. Amendments to the Constitution enter into force immediately after their adoption in the Assembly of the Republic of Kosovo.

Article 145   [Continuity of International Agreements and Applicable Legislation]

1. International agreements and other acts relating to international cooperation that are in effect on the day this Constitution enters into force will continue to be respected until such agreements or acts are renegotiated or withdrawn from in accordance with their terms or until they are superseded by new international agreements or acts covering the same subject areas and adopted pursuant to this Constitution.

2. Legislation applicable on the date of the entry into force of this Constitution shall continue to apply to the extent it is in conformity with this Constitution until repealed, superseded or amended in accordance with this Constitution.

Chapter XIV   Transitional Provisions

Article 146   [International Civilian Representative]

Notwithstanding any provision of this Constitution:

1. The International Civilian Representative and other international organizations and actors mandated under the Comprehensive Proposal for the Kosovo Status Settlement dated 26 March 2007 have the mandate and powers set forth under the said Comprehensive Proposal, including the legal capacity and privileges and immunities set forth therein.

2. All authorities in the Republic of Kosovo shall cooperate fully with the International Civilian Representative, other international organizations and actors mandated under the Comprehensive Proposal for the Kosovo Status Settlement dated 26 March 2007 and shall, *inter alia*, give effect to their decisions or acts.

Article 147   [Final Authority of the International Civilian Representative]

Notwithstanding any provision of this Constitution, the International Civilian Representative shall, in accordance with the Comprehensive Proposal for the Kosovo Status Settlement dated 26 March 2007, be the final authority in Kosovo regarding interpretation of the civilian aspects of the said Comprehensive Proposal. No Republic of Kosovo authority shall have jurisdiction to review, diminish or otherwise restrict the mandate, powers and obligations referred to in Article 146 and this Article.

Article 148   [Transitional Provisions for the Assembly of Kosovo]

1. For the first two (2) electoral mandates, the Assembly of Kosovo shall have twenty (20) seats reserved for representation of Communities that are not in the majority in Kosovo, as follows: Ten (10) seats shall be allocated to the parties, coalitions, citizens' initiatives and independent candidates having declared themselves representing the Kosovo Serb Community and ten (10) seats shall be allocated to other Communities as follows: the Roma community, one (1) seat; the Ashkali community, one (1) seat; the Egyptian community, one (1) seat; and one (1) additional seat will be awarded to either the Roma, the Ashkali or the Egyptian community with the highest overall votes; the Bosniak community, three (3) seats; the Turkish community, two (2) seats; and the Gorani community, one (1) seat. Any seats gained through elections shall be in addition to the ten
(10) reserved seats allocated to the Kosovo Serb Community and other Communities respectively.

2. Notwithstanding paragraph 1 of this Article, the mandate existing at the time of entry into force of this Constitution will be deemed to be the first electoral mandate of the Assembly, provided that such mandate continues for a period of at least two (2) years from the date of entry into force of this Constitution.

Article 149   [Initial Adoption of Laws of Vital Interest]

Notwithstanding the provisions of Article 81 of this Constitution, the laws of vital interest enumerated therein shall be initially adopted by the majority vote of the deputies of the Assembly present and voting.

Article 150   [Appointment Process for Judges and Prosecutors]

1. The comprehensive, Kosovo-wide review of the suitability of all applicants for permanent appointments, until the retirement age determined by law, as judges and public prosecutors in Kosovo shall continue to be carried out in accordance with Administrative Direction 2008/02 and shall not be affected by the termination of the United Nations Mission in Kosovo (UNMIK)'s mandate or the entry into force of this Constitution.

2. All successful candidates who have been appointed or reappointed as judges and prosecutors by the Special Representative of the Secretary General (SRSG) as part of the Appointment Process shall continue to serve in their posts until the natural expiration of their appointment, or until such time as they are dismissed in accordance with law.

3. The Independent Judicial and Prosecutorial Commission shall submit recommendations on candidates for appointment or reappointment as judges and prosecutors in writing to the Kosovo Judicial Council, which shall exercise final authority to propose to the President of Kosovo candidates for appointment or reappointment as judges and prosecutors.

4. All successful candidates who have been appointed or reappointed as judges and prosecutors by the President of Kosovo on the proposal of the Kosovo Judicial Council as part of the Appointment Process shall continue to serve in their posts until the natural expiration of their appointment, or until such time as they are dismissed in accordance with law.

5. Notwithstanding Article 105 of this Constitution, the mandate of all judges and prosecutors successfully completing the appointment process set forth in this Article and who have exercised the function for at least two years prior to appointment pursuant to this article is permanent until the retirement age as determined by law or unless removed in accordance with law.

Article 151   [Temporary Composition of Kosovo Judicial Council]

Until the end of the international supervision of the implementation of the Comprehensive Proposal for Kosovo Status Settlement, dated 26 March 2007, the Kosovo Judicial Council shall be composed as follows:

1. Five (5) members shall consist of the Kosovan members of the Independent Judicial and Prosecutorial Commission who have been vetted by the Independent Judicial and Prosecutorial Commission as part of Phases 1 and 2 of the Appointment Process, in accordance with Administrative Direction 2008/02. Of these five (5) members, one (1)

judge and one (1) prosecutor, randomly selected, shall serve on the Kosovo Judicial Council until the natural expiration of their existing mandates, at which time they shall be replaced by one (1) judge and one (1) prosecutor vetted by the Independent Judicial and Prosecutorial Commission and elected by their peers following methods intended to ensure the widest representation of the judiciary and prosecutorial service. The remaining two (2) judges and one (1) prosecutor, from among the five Kosovan Independent Judicial and Prosecutorial Commission members, shall serve on the Kosovo Judicial Council for an additional one (1) year term after the natural expiration of their existing mandates, at which time they shall be replaced by the same procedure as their former Independent Judicial and Prosecutorial Commission colleagues. In the event that an entity responsible for matters related to the appointment, disciplining and dismissal of prosecutors were established, all five remaining members of the Kosovo Judicial Council shall be judges.

2. The remaining eight (8) members of the Council shall be elected by the Assembly of Kosovo as set forth by this Constitution, except that two (2) out of the four (4) members elected by deputies holding seats attributed during the general distribution of seats shall be international members selected by the International Civilian Representative on the proposal of the European Security and Defense Policy Mission. One of the international members shall be a judge.

Article 152   [Temporary Composition of the Constitutional Court]

Until the end of the international supervision of the implementation of the Comprehensive Proposal for Kosovo Status Settlement, dated 26 March 2007, the Constitutional Court shall be composed as follows:

1. Six (6) out of nine (9) judges shall be appointed by the President of the Republic of Kosovo on the proposal of the Assembly.

2. Of the six (6) judges two (2) judges shall serve for a non-renewable term of three (3) years, two (2) judges shall serve for a non-renewable term of six (6) years, and two (2) judges shall serve for a non-renewable term of nine (9) years. Mandates of initial period judges shall be chosen by lot by the President of the Republic of Kosovo immediately after their appointment.

3. Of the six (6) judges, four (4) shall be elected by a two-thirds (2/3) vote of the deputies of Assembly present and voting. Two (2) shall be elected by majority of the deputies of the Assembly present and voting including the consent of the majority of the deputies of the Assembly holding seats reserved or guaranteed for representatives of Communities that are not in the majority in Kosovo.

4. Three (3) international judges shall be appointed by the International Civilian Representative, upon consultation with the President of the European Court of Human Rights. The three (3) international judges shall not be citizens of Kosovo or any neighboring country.

5. The International Civilian Representative shall determine when the mandates of the international judges expire and the judges shall be replaced as set forth by the Constitution.

Article 153 [International Military Presence]

Notwithstanding any provision of this Constitution, the International Military Presence has the mandate and powers set forth under the relevant international instruments including United Nations Security Council Resolution 1244 and the Comprehensive Proposal for the Kosovo Status Settlement dated 26 March 2007. The Head of the International Military Presence shall, in accordance with the Comprehensive Proposal for the Kosovo Status Settlement dated 26 March 2007, be the final authority in theatre regarding interpretation of those aspects of the said Settlement that refer to the International Military Presence. No Republic of Kosovo authority shall have jurisdiction to review, diminish or otherwise restrict the mandate, powers and obligations referred to in this Article.

Article 154 [Kosovo Protection Corps]

The Kosovo Protection Corps shall be dissolved within one year after entry into force of this Constitution. Until such dissolution, the International Military Presence, in consultation with the International Civilian Representative and the Republic of Kosovo, shall exercise executive authority over the Kosovo Protection Corps and shall decide on the schedule of its dissolution.

Article 155 [Citizenship]

1. All legal residents of the Republic of Kosovo as of the date of the adoption of this Constitution have the right to citizenship of the Republic of Kosovo.

2. The Republic of Kosovo recognizes the right of all citizens of the former Federal Republic of Yugoslavia habitually residing in Kosovo on 1 January 1998 and their direct descendants to Republic of Kosovo citizenship regardless of their current residence and of any other citizenship they may hold.

Article 156 [Refugees and Internally Displaced Persons]

The Republic of Kosovo shall promote and facilitate the safe and dignified return of refugees and internally displaced persons and assist them in recovering their property and possession.

Article 157 [Auditor-General of Kosovo]

Until the end of the international supervision of the implementation of the Comprehensive Proposal for Kosovo Status Settlement, dated 26 March 2007, the Auditor-General of the Republic of Kosovo shall be an international appointed by the International Civilian Representative.

Article 158 [Central Banking Authority]

Until the end of the international supervision of the implementation of the Comprehensive Proposal for Kosovo Status Settlement, dated 26 March 2007, the Governor of the Central

Bank of the Republic of Kosovo shall be appointed by the President of the Republic of Kosovo following consent by the International Civilian Representative.

Article 159 [Socially Owned Enterprises and Property]

1. All enterprises that were wholly or partly in social ownership prior to the effective date of this Constitution shall be privatized in accordance with law.

2. All socially owned interests in property and enterprises in Kosovo shall be owned by the Republic of Kosovo.

Article 160 [Publicly Owned Enterprises]

1. The Republic of Kosovo shall own all enterprises in the Republic of Kosovo that are Publicly Owned Enterprises. All obligations related to such ownership rights shall be the obligations of the Republic of Kosovo. The Government of Kosovo may privatize, concession or lease a Publicly Owned Enterprise as provided by law.

2. The ownership rights in a Publicly Owned Enterprise that provides services only in a specific municipality or in a limited number of municipalities shall be the ownership rights of the concerned municipality or municipalities. Obligations related to such ownership rights shall be the obligations of the concerned municipality or municipalities. The Assembly of Kosovo shall, by law, identify such Publicly Owned Enterprise and the concerned municipality or municipalities having ownership rights and related obligations with respect thereto. If authorized by law, the concerned municipality or municipalities may privatize, concession or lease such a Publicly Owned Enterprise.

Article 161 [Transition of Institutions]

1. Except where the Constitution provides a different transition, all powers, responsibilities and obligations of the institutions foreseen by this Constitution are immediately vested in those institutions on the day of entry into force of this Constitution. The mandate of each institution as established prior to the entry into force of this Constitution remains intact and unchanged until its natural expiration or the next elections.

2. Until the first parliamentary elections following entry into force of this Constitution, the Presidency of the Assembly will remain in place with those powers foreseen under its existing mandate. As of the constitutive session of the first Assembly following the entry into force of this Constitution, the Presidency of the Assembly will be restructured to comply with the terms of this Constitution.

3. The provisions of Article 70.3(3) shall not apply until the constitutive session of the Assembly following the first parliamentary elections following the entry into force of this Constitution.

4. Until the establishment of the Kosovo Prosecutorial Council, its functions and responsibilities will be exercised by the Kosovo Judicial Council.

Article 162   [Effective Date]

This Constitution shall enter into force and effect on 15 June 2008.

Notes